Italy Travel Guide

The Essential Pocket Guide to Discover Hidden Gems and Authentic Experiences in the Land of La Dolce Vita.

Ginevra Costa

© Copyright 2024 by Ginevra Costa
All rights reserved

This document is geared towards providing exact and reliable information with regards to the topic and issue covered. The publication is sold with the idea that the publisher is not required to render accounting, officially permitted, or otherwise, qualified services. If advice is necessary, legal or professional, a practiced individual in the profession should be ordered.

From a Declaration of Principles which was accepted and approved equally by a Committee of the American Bar Association and a Committee of Publishers and Associations.

In no way is it legal to reproduce, duplicate, or transmit any part of this document in either electronic means or in printed format. Recording of this publication is strictly prohibited and any storage of this document is not allowed unless with written permission from the publisher. All rights reserved.

The information provided herein is stated to be truthful and consistent, in that any liability, in terms of inattention or otherwise, by any usage or abuse of any policies, processes, or directions contained within is the solitary and utter responsibility of the recipient reader. Under no circumstances will any legal responsibility or blame be held against the publisher for any reparation, damages, or monetary loss due to the information herein, either directly or indirectly.

Respective authors own all copyrights not held by the publisher.

The information herein is offered for informational purposes solely, and is universal as so. The presentation of the information is without contract or any type of guarantee assurance.

The trademarks that are used are without any consent, and the publication of the trademark is without permission or backing by the trademark owner. All trademarks and brands within this book are for clarifying purposes only and are the owned by the owners themselves, not affiliated with this document.

TABLE OF CONTENTS

1. Introduction to La Dolce Vita 5
   1.1.   The Essence of Italian Living 5
   1.2.   How to Use This Guide 7
   1.3.   Brief History of Italy 9
   1.4.   Italian Culture and Customs 12
   1.5.   Planning Your Italian Adventure 14

2. Navigating Italy 18
   2.1. Transportation Options 18
   2.2. Italian Phrases for Travelers 21
   2.3. Accommodation Tips 23
   2.4. Budgeting for Your Trip 25
   2.5. Safety and Health Information 28
   2.6. Off-the-Beaten-Path Travel Strategies 30

3. Hidden Gems of Northern Italy 34
   3.1. Undiscovered Treasures of Venice 34
   3.2. Lake Como's Secret Spots 36
   3.3. Turin: Italy's Underrated Gem 39
   3.4. The Dolomites: Beyond the Ski Resorts 42
   3.5. Emilia-Romagna's Culinary Secrets 44
   3.6. Cinque Terre: Away from the Crowds 47
   3.7. Lesser-Known Tuscan Villages 50

4. Central Italy's Authentic Experiences 54
   4.1. Rome: Beyond the Colosseum 54
   4.2. Florence's Artisan Workshops 56
   4.3. Umbria: The Green Heart of Italy 59
   4.4. Le Marche: Italy's Best-Kept Secret 61
   4.5. Abruzzo's Wild Beauty 63
   4.6. Authentic Farmstays and Agriturismos 66

5. Southern Italy and Islands Unveiled 71
   5.1. Naples: Hidden Alleys and Underground Cities 71
   5.2. Puglia's Trulli and Masserie 73
   5.3. Calabria's Rugged Coastlines 75

5.4. Sicily: Ancient Traditions and Modern Flair...78

5.5. Sardinia's Interior: A Step Back in Time 80

5.6. The Aeolian Islands: Volcanic Wonders...83

6. Practical Tips for Authentic Italian Experiences 87

6.1. Connecting with Locals 87

6.2. Using Technology to Discover Hidden Gems 89

6.3. Seasonal Events and Festivals 91

6.4. Nightlife Beyond the Tourist Areas 93

6.5. Shopping Like a Local..95

6.6. Dealing with Unexpected Situations 97

6.7. Resources for Further Exploration 100

BONUS 1: 10 travel tips "that can save the day" during an italian adventure 103

BONUS 2: 50 essential italian phrases for your daily travel needs...................................... 104

BONUS 3: Printable travel journal 105

1. INTRODUCTION TO LA DOLCE VITA

1.1. The Essence of Italian Living

La Dolce Vita, the quintessential Italian way of life, captures a unique blend of leisurely elegance, passionate pursuits, and a deep appreciation for life's simple pleasures. This essence is woven into the fabric of Italy, from bustling piazzas to tranquil countryside retreats. In understanding the essence of Italian living, one must first grasp the importance of community and family. Italians are social by nature, often gathering in vibrant groups to share meals, stories, and laughter. The shared table is a sacred space where bonds are strengthened over hearty plates of pasta and glasses of robust wine. It's not just about the food, though it plays a central role; it's about connection, celebration, and the warmth of human interaction.

Italian living thrives on a slower, more deliberate pace that encourages savoring each moment. This is evident in the daily ritual of the "passeggiata," an evening stroll where locals amble through town squares and along cobblestone streets, greeting neighbors and pausing for a gelato or espresso. It's a time to unwind, reflect, and enjoy the beauty of one's surroundings. The art of living well in Italy is not rushed or hurried but enjoyed in a relaxed manner that prioritizes mindfulness and presence.

The Italian aesthetic, a harmonious blend of art, history, and nature, is another pillar of this lifestyle. Italians are inherently drawn to beauty, evident in their meticulously maintained gardens, ornate architecture, and fashion that seamlessly combines style with comfort. This appreciation for beauty extends to their language, rich with expressive gestures and melodic tones that convey emotion effortlessly. Whether it's the rustic charm of a Tuscan villa or the opulence of a Roman palazzo, the Italian eye for design is both sophisticated and inviting.

Food, as mentioned, is a cornerstone of Italian life, but it's more than just sustenance; it's an art form, a tradition, and a source of pride. Italians have a profound respect for their culinary heritage, with recipes passed down through generations. Each region boasts its own specialties, from the creamy risottos of the north to the fiery spices of the south. Markets brimming with fresh produce, cheese, and cured meats are a testament to the country's commitment to quality and authenticity. Cooking is a communal act, often involving family members of all ages in the preparation of meals, fostering a sense of unity and continuity.

Beyond the tangible aspects of Italian living lies a deeper philosophical approach to life—one that values passion, resilience, and adaptability. Italians embrace a "joie de vivre" that celebrates both life's triumphs and challenges. The concept of "bella figura," or making a good impression, speaks to a broader mindset that emphasizes dignity, respect, and personal responsibility. It's about presenting oneself with confidence and grace, regardless of circumstances, and finding joy even in adversity.

The natural landscape of Italy, with its rolling hills, serene lakes, and dramatic coastlines, is an integral part of this lifestyle. Nature provides a backdrop for recreation and relaxation, whether it's hiking in the Dolomites, sailing along the Amalfi Coast, or simply enjoying a picnic in a sun-dappled vineyard. Italians have a close relationship with the land, evident in their sustainable agricultural practices and dedication to preserving the environment for future generations.

Italian festivals and traditions, deeply rooted in history and culture, offer a glimpse into the communal spirit that defines the nation. These events, ranging from religious processions to secular celebrations, are marked by music, dance, and culinary indulgence. They serve as reminders of the shared heritage that unites Italians, fostering a sense of identity and belonging. Participation in these festivities is not merely an obligation but a joyous expression of cultural pride and unity.

Art and creativity are woven into the fabric of Italian life, with a rich legacy of contributions to the world of music, literature, and visual arts. From the masterpieces of Michelangelo and Da Vinci to the modern works of contemporary artists, Italy's cultural landscape is a testament to its enduring influence and innovation. Italians are encouraged to cultivate their artistic talents, whether through formal education or personal exploration, as a means of self-expression and enrichment.

In the realm of relationships, Italians place a high value on loyalty, trust, and intimacy. Friendships are cherished, often lasting a lifetime, and family ties are considered unbreakable. The concept of "amore," or love, transcends romantic relationships, encompassing a broader sense of affection and care for all aspects of life. This emotional depth is reflected in the way Italians interact, with a warmth and sincerity that foster genuine connections.

The Italian approach to work-life balance is another defining feature of this lifestyle. While Italians are dedicated and hardworking, they also prioritize leisure and relaxation. The importance of "dolce far niente," or the sweetness of doing nothing, is a reminder to take time for oneself to recharge and rejuvenate.

Whether it's enjoying a leisurely lunch, taking a midday siesta, or spending a weekend in the countryside, Italians understand the value of rest and relaxation in maintaining overall well-being.

In essence, Italian living is about embracing life with open arms and an open heart. It's about finding beauty in the everyday, cherishing relationships, and living with passion and purpose. This approach to life, deeply rooted in tradition yet open to change, offers a timeless model for finding fulfillment and happiness in the modern world. By immersing oneself in the rhythms and rituals of Italian life, one can discover a richer, more meaningful way of being, where every moment is savored and every experience is treasured.

1.2. How to Use This Guide

Embarking on a journey through Italy, with its myriad of experiences, requires a guide that not only informs but also inspires. This guide is designed to be your compass as you navigate the diverse landscapes, rich histories, and vibrant cultures of this enchanting country. Its comprehensive structure, focused on uncovering hidden gems and authentic experiences, will allow you to craft a unique and personal Italian adventure.

Begin by familiarizing yourself with the guide's layout. Each section is meticulously organized to cover different aspects of Italy—from the bustling cities to the serene countryside, from the culinary delights to the artistic wonders. By understanding the flow of the guide, you can easily access the information you need, whether you're planning your itinerary or seeking spontaneous adventures.

As you dive into each chapter, pay attention to the detailed descriptions and insights that capture the essence of each destination. These narratives are intended to evoke a sense of place, allowing you to imagine the sights, sounds, and flavors that await you. Use these vivid portrayals to prioritize your must-see locations, while also keeping an open mind to the unexpected discoveries that often make travel so memorable.

The guide is not just about listing places to visit; it also offers practical advice to enhance your journey. For instance, transportation tips will help you navigate Italy's intricate network of trains, buses, and regional flights. You'll find suggestions for choosing accommodations that align with your preferences, whether you seek the luxury of a boutique hotel or the charm of a rustic agriturismo. This practical information is meant to simplify your travel planning, so you can focus on immersing yourself in the Italian experience.

Language is an integral part of engaging with Italy's culture. While many Italians speak English, especially in tourist areas, learning a few basic Italian phrases can enrich your interactions and show respect for the local customs. This guide includes a selection of essential phrases tailored for travelers, from ordering food to asking for directions. Using these phrases can lead to more meaningful exchanges and perhaps even a new friendship or two.

Budgeting is another crucial aspect addressed within these pages. Italy offers a range of experiences to suit various financial plans, from opulent splurges to affordable delights. The guide provides strategies for managing your expenses without compromising on quality, such as finding hidden dining spots where locals eat or exploring lesser-known attractions that offer free or reduced admission. With this guidance, you can enjoy the best of Italy without breaking the bank.

Safety and health are priorities that cannot be overlooked. The guide includes important information on staying safe, from understanding local laws to being aware of common scams. Tips for maintaining your health while traveling, such as the location of pharmacies or the availability of medical services, are also covered. This section aims to equip you with the knowledge needed to handle unforeseen situations calmly and effectively.

To truly appreciate Italy, consider embracing off-the-beaten-path strategies that take you beyond the typical tourist trail. The guide highlights lesser-known destinations and activities that offer a more intimate glimpse of Italian life. By venturing into these hidden corners, you can experience the authenticity that makes Italy so captivating. Whether it's a secluded beach, a quaint village festival, or a family-run vineyard, these discoveries will add depth and texture to your travel narrative.

As you explore, remember that this guide is a tool to enhance your journey, not dictate it. Allow yourself the freedom to wander and adapt your plans as you go. Some of the most cherished travel memories arise from unplanned adventures and serendipitous encounters. Use the guide as a foundation, but let your curiosity and instincts lead you to new experiences.

In addition to practical advice, this guide encourages you to connect with the heart of Italy—its people. Italians are known for their warmth and hospitality, and forming genuine connections can deepen your appreciation of the culture. Whether it's chatting with a shopkeeper, participating in a local event, or sharing a meal with a family, these interactions will enrich your understanding of Italian life and create lasting memories.

Technology can be a valuable ally in your travels, and the guide offers suggestions on using apps and online resources to discover hidden gems. From digital maps to local blogs, these tools can provide real-time information and insider tips. However, it's important to balance screen time with real-world experiences. Use technology to enhance your journey, but don't let it distract from the beauty around you.

Lastly, approach your Italian adventure with a spirit of openness and respect. Each region of Italy has its own customs and traditions, and embracing these differences will make your journey more rewarding. Whether it's understanding the etiquette of dining or participating in a regional festival, showing respect for local ways will enhance your travel experience and leave a positive impression.

This guide is your companion in navigating the wonders of Italy. By utilizing its resources thoughtfully, you can craft a journey that not only fulfills your travel dreams but also offers a deeper connection to this remarkable land. With each page, you'll uncover new opportunities to explore, learn, and grow—creating a tapestry of experiences that will stay with you long after you've returned home.

1.3. Brief History of Italy

Italy, a land steeped in history and culture, has long been a focal point of human civilization, with its narrative stretching back thousands of years. From the ancient tribes that first settled the peninsula to the influential city-states of the

Renaissance, Italy's past is as varied as its landscapes. Understanding this historical tapestry is essential for anyone seeking to grasp the essence of this fascinating country.

The story begins with the prehistoric tribes that roamed the Italian peninsula. The Etruscans, one of the earliest significant cultures, left behind a legacy of art, architecture, and urban planning that would influence their successors. Meanwhile, Greek settlers established colonies in southern Italy and Sicily, bringing with them their rich traditions of philosophy, politics, and the arts, which left an indelible mark on the region.

The rise of Rome marked a turning point in Italy's history. Founded in 753 BC, Rome evolved from a small settlement to a sprawling empire that dominated the Mediterranean world. The Romans were master builders, engineers, and administrators, known for their roads, aqueducts, and monumental architecture. The Pax Romana, a period of relative peace and stability, allowed for the flourishing of arts, culture, and trade. However, the decline of the Roman Empire in the 5th century AD led to a period of fragmentation and chaos, as various barbarian tribes, including the Ostrogoths and Lombards, carved out territories.

The Middle Ages in Italy were characterized by the rise of powerful city-states, each vying for dominance. Cities like Venice, Florence, and Genoa became centers of commerce and culture, their wealth fueling artistic and intellectual endeavors. This period saw the emergence of the Italian Renaissance, a cultural rebirth that produced some of history's greatest artists, thinkers, and scientists. Figures such as Leonardo da Vinci, Michelangelo, and Galileo Galilei pushed the boundaries of human knowledge and creativity, leaving a lasting legacy.

The Renaissance also witnessed the development of new political and social structures. The Medici family in Florence, for example, exemplified the fusion of political power with cultural patronage, their influence extending beyond Italy's borders. The Renaissance values of humanism and individualism would go on to shape European thought and society.

The 16th century brought new challenges as Italy became a battleground for European powers. The Italian Wars saw Spain, France, and the Holy Roman Empire fight for control over the peninsula, leading to a period of foreign domination. Despite this, Italy remained a vibrant cultural hub, its cities continuing to produce influential works of art, music, and literature.

The 19th century was a time of upheaval and transformation. The Napoleonic Wars and the subsequent Congress of Vienna left Italy fragmented, but the seeds of nationalism had been sown. The Risorgimento, or the Italian unification movement, gained momentum as figures like Giuseppe Garibaldi, Camillo Cavour, and Victor Emmanuel II worked towards a unified Italy. In 1861, the Kingdom of Italy was officially proclaimed, marking a new chapter in the nation's history.

The 20th century brought both triumph and tragedy. Italy's involvement in World War I resulted in significant territorial gains, but the post-war period was marked by economic hardship and political instability. This turmoil paved the way for the rise of Benito Mussolini and the Fascist regime, which promised to restore Italy's glory but led the country into the devastation of World War II.

Following the war, Italy emerged as a republic, embarking on a path of reconstruction and modernization. The post-war economic miracle transformed the country into an industrial powerhouse, with rapid urbanization and infrastructure development. Italy became a founding member of the European Union, playing a crucial role in shaping the continent's future.

Today, Italy is a nation that balances its rich historical heritage with a dynamic present. Its cities are living museums, where ancient ruins stand alongside modern architecture, and its cultural contributions continue to influence the world. From its vibrant fashion industry to its renowned cuisine, Italy remains a beacon of creativity and innovation.

This historical journey, spanning millennia, has crafted a nation of contrasts and complexity. Italy's past informs its present, offering visitors a deep and multifaceted experience. Exploring its history is not just about understanding dates and events but about connecting with the people and stories that have shaped this remarkable land. Each era, from the ancient to the modern, has left its mark, contributing to the rich tapestry that is Italy today.

1.4. Italian Culture and Customs

Italian culture, a mosaic of centuries-old traditions and modern influences, is as diverse as the regions that make up this historically rich nation. It's a vibrant tapestry where art, food, fashion, and family play central roles, creating a unique lifestyle that continues to captivate travelers and scholars alike. Understanding these elements is essential for anyone wishing to truly experience Italy beyond its picturesque landscapes.

Family is the cornerstone of Italian society, with strong bonds that often extend beyond the nuclear unit to include extended relatives. Sundays are typically reserved for large family gatherings, where multiple generations come together to share meals and stories. This sense of familial closeness fosters a network of support and loyalty, with family members often living in close proximity or even under the same roof. In Italy, family is not just important; it is everything.

Mealtime in Italy is an event in itself, reflecting the country's deep-rooted appreciation for culinary arts. Italians approach food with a reverence that borders on the spiritual, often emphasizing the use of fresh, seasonal ingredients. A typical Italian meal is a multi-course affair, beginning with antipasti, followed by a primo of pasta or risotto, a secondo of meat or fish, and concluding with dolce, a sweet indulgence. Meals are leisurely, an opportunity to savor flavors and engage in lively conversation. Wine flows freely, enhancing the communal atmosphere and adding to the conviviality.

Fashion is another pillar of Italian culture, with cities like Milan serving as global trendsetters. Italians take pride in their appearance, often opting for elegant yet understated clothing that exudes sophistication. The concept of "bella figura," or making a good impression, extends beyond attire to encompass overall demeanor and behavior. This cultural emphasis on aesthetics and presentation is evident in everything from architecture to everyday interactions, where elegance and grace are prized.

Art and architecture are intrinsic to Italy's identity, with the country boasting an unparalleled wealth of cultural treasures. From the frescoes of the Sistine Chapel to the canals of Venice, Italy's artistic heritage is a testament to its historical significance. The Renaissance, born in Florence, revolutionized art with its focus on humanism and realism, producing masterpieces that continue to inspire. Today, Italy remains a hub for artists and architects, blending traditional techniques with contemporary innovation.

Religion, predominantly Roman Catholicism, plays a significant role in shaping Italian customs and values. The majority of Italians celebrate religious festivals, which often coincide with important cultural events. These festivals, marked by processions, music, and feasting, underscore the communal spirit and historical continuity of Italian towns and cities. The Vatican City, located within Rome, serves as the spiritual heart of Catholicism, drawing pilgrims and tourists from around the globe.

Language is a vital component of Italian culture, characterized by its melodic flow and expressive gestures. While Italian is the official language, regional dialects add a layer of diversity, reflecting the country's fragmented past. Communication is often animated, with hand gestures complementing verbal expression, creating a dynamic exchange that is both engaging and revealing.

Hospitality is deeply ingrained in the Italian psyche, with a natural warmth and generosity extended to guests and strangers alike. Italians are known for their openness, often welcoming visitors into their homes for a meal or a coffee. This hospitality extends to the service industry, where interactions are typically cordial and attentive, adding to the overall enjoyment of any visit to Italy.

Leisure and recreation are valued aspects of Italian life, with a focus on balancing work and relaxation. The concept of "dolce far niente," or the sweetness of doing nothing, encapsulates the Italian approach to leisure, promoting the idea that taking time to relax and enjoy life's simple pleasures is integral to well-being. Whether it's sipping espresso at a café or strolling through a sun-drenched piazza, Italians embrace leisure as a necessary and enriching part of life.

Sports, especially soccer, are a passion that unites Italians across regions and generations. Serie A matches draw fervent crowds, with fans displaying unwavering loyalty to their teams. Beyond professional sports, Italians enjoy a variety of recreational activities, from cycling through the countryside to skiing in the Alps, reflecting the diverse natural landscapes that the country offers.

Italian culture is a rich tapestry that weaves together history, art, cuisine, and community. It is a culture that celebrates beauty in all its forms, from the flavors of a home-cooked meal to the intricate details of a fresco. By embracing these customs and values, one gains a deeper appreciation for Italy and its people, experiencing the essence of a nation that has long been a beacon of civilization and creativity. This understanding not only enriches travel experiences but also offers insights into the timeless appeal of Italian life, a way of living that continues to inspire and captivate the world.

1.5. Planning Your Italian Adventure

Planning your Italian adventure is an exhilarating endeavor, filled with the promise of discovering a country that offers an endless array of experiences. From the enchanting canals of Venice to the vibrant streets of Naples, Italy is a treasure trove waiting to be explored. Crafting the perfect itinerary requires a balance of must-see attractions and hidden gems, ensuring that each day brings new delights and memories.

Start by identifying your priorities and interests. Italy's diverse regions offer something for everyone: art enthusiasts may gravitate towards Florence's galleries, history buffs might find Rome's ancient ruins irresistible, while foodies could explore the culinary delights of Bologna. Consider what excites you the most and let that guide your planning. This personal approach ensures your journey is tailored to your passions, creating a more fulfilling experience.

Time is a crucial factor in planning your Italian escapade. Italy's wealth of attractions can be overwhelming, and it's important to pace yourself to fully enjoy each moment. Allocate at least a few days to each major city, allowing time to explore both famous landmarks and local neighborhoods. For instance, while in Florence, dedicate a day to marvel at the Uffizi Gallery, but also wander through the Oltrarno district, known for its artisan workshops and charming cafes. By striking a balance between sightseeing and relaxation, you create a more enjoyable and less rushed itinerary.

Accommodation choices play a significant role in shaping your travel experience. Italy offers a wide range of options, from luxurious hotels to quaint bed-and-breakfasts. Consider staying in locally-owned properties that provide a more authentic experience, such as an agriturismo in Tuscany or a family-run guesthouse in Sicily. These accommodations often offer insights into local culture and traditions, enhancing your connection to the region. Booking in advance, especially during peak travel seasons, ensures you have a comfortable base from which to explore.

Transportation within Italy is an adventure in itself. The country's efficient train network connects major cities and picturesque towns, offering a scenic and stress-free way to travel. High-speed trains whisk you between Rome and Milan in just a few hours, while regional trains provide access to lesser-known destinations. For more remote areas, consider renting a car, which grants the freedom to explore at your own pace. Navigating Italy's roads can be challenging, with narrow streets and local driving customs, but the flexibility it offers is often worth the effort.

Language, while not a barrier, can enhance your experience if embraced. Learning a few basic Italian phrases can enrich your interactions and show respect for the local culture. Italians appreciate efforts to speak their language, no matter how rudimentary, and it often leads to warmer connections and helpful tips. Carry a pocket phrasebook or use language apps to assist in communication, particularly in rural areas where English may be less commonly spoken.

Cultural events and festivals offer unique insights into Italian life, and planning your trip around these occasions can add a special dimension to your adventure. From the vibrant Carnival of Venice to the historical Palio di Siena, these events showcase local traditions, music, and cuisine. Researching festival dates and incorporating them into your itinerary allows you to witness Italy's rich cultural tapestry firsthand. Keep in mind that festivals can also mean increased crowds and prices, so plan accordingly.

Budgeting is an essential aspect of travel planning, and Italy offers a range of experiences to suit different financial plans. While it's easy to splurge on gourmet meals and designer shopping, there are also plenty of affordable options that don't compromise on quality. Seek out trattorias and osterias frequented by locals, where you can enjoy authentic Italian cuisine at reasonable prices. Many museums and attractions offer discounted or free entry on certain days, so take advantage of these opportunities to stretch your budget further.

Packing for Italy requires consideration of the country's varied climates and cultural norms. Lightweight, breathable clothing is ideal for summer months, while layers are essential for cooler seasons. Italians tend to dress stylishly, particularly in urban areas, so opting for smart-casual attire can help you blend in. Comfortable walking shoes are a must, as exploring Italy often involves traversing cobblestone streets and uneven terrain. Additionally, pack a reusable water bottle to stay hydrated and reduce plastic waste.

Safety and security should always be a priority, and Italy is generally a safe destination for travelers. However, like any popular tourist location, it's important to remain vigilant, particularly in crowded areas where pickpocketing can occur. Keep valuables secure, use hotel safes, and be cautious of scams targeting tourists. Familiarize yourself with local emergency numbers and healthcare facilities, ensuring you're prepared for any unforeseen circumstances.

Finally, approach your Italian adventure with an open mind and a flexible attitude. While planning is essential, leaving room for spontaneity can lead to some of the most rewarding experiences. Allow yourself to wander off the beaten path, engage with locals, and embrace the unexpected. Whether it's a hidden trattoria discovered by chance or a conversation with a friendly shopkeeper, these moments often become the highlights of your journey.

By thoughtfully planning your Italian adventure, you create a framework that allows for both structure and surprise. Each decision, from where to stay to how to travel, shapes your experience, turning your trip into a personal narrative of exploration and discovery. With this guide in hand, you are well-equipped to embark on an unforgettable journey through the heart of Italy, where every day brings new stories and memories to cherish.

2. NAVIGATING ITALY

2.1. Transportation Options

Italy's transportation network is a complex yet fascinating tapestry, blending modern efficiency with historical charm. To truly appreciate and navigate this intricate system, understanding the various options available is essential for any traveler. From the iconic trains that traverse breathtaking landscapes to the winding roads perfect for a leisurely drive, Italy offers a multitude of ways to explore its treasures.

Trains are perhaps the most iconic and convenient mode of transportation in Italy, connecting major cities and scenic towns with remarkable ease. The country's train system is divided into high-speed rail, regional trains, and scenic routes, each offering a unique experience. High-speed options like the Frecciarossa and Italo connect cities such as Rome, Milan, Florence, and Naples in mere hours, providing a comfortable and rapid means of travel. These trains are equipped with modern amenities, including Wi-Fi, dining services, and spacious seating, ensuring a pleasant journey.

For those seeking a more leisurely pace, regional trains offer access to picturesque towns and lesser-known destinations. These trains are ideal for exploring areas off the beaten path, granting a glimpse into Italy's diverse landscapes and cultures. While regional trains may lack the luxury of high-speed services, they more than make up for it with affordability and charm. It's worth noting that some regional routes can be quite popular, so booking in advance is recommended, especially during peak travel seasons.

Another enchanting way to experience Italy is by embarking on one of its scenic train journeys. Routes like the Bernina Express, which traverses the Alps, or the Circumetnea, encircling Mount Etna in Sicily, provide breathtaking views and an unforgettable travel experience. These journeys often highlight the diverse natural beauty of Italy, from snow-capped mountains to verdant vineyards, creating memories that last a lifetime.

Buses offer an alternative means of transportation, particularly useful for reaching destinations not accessible by train. Italy's extensive bus network connects rural areas and smaller towns, making it an essential option for travelers exploring the country's hidden gems. Companies like FlixBus and SITA operate routes throughout Italy, providing a cost-effective solution for those on a budget. While bus travel can be slower than trains, it offers flexibility and access to regions that might otherwise be missed.

For those who crave independence and flexibility, renting a car is an attractive option. Italy's diverse terrain, from the rolling hills of Tuscany to the dramatic coastline of the Amalfi Coast, is best appreciated at your own pace. Driving allows you to explore remote villages, discover local eateries, and enjoy the freedom to create your own itinerary. However, it's important to be aware of Italy's driving regulations, including the requirement for an International Driving Permit for non-EU citizens and the presence of ZTL (Zona a Traffico Limitato) zones in many city centers, which restrict vehicle access to reduce congestion.

Navigating Italy's roads can be both thrilling and challenging, with narrow streets, sharp turns, and enthusiastic local drivers. Travelers should be prepared for varying road conditions and the occasional toll road. Nevertheless, the rewards of traversing Italy by car often outweigh the challenges, offering a unique perspective on the country's diverse regions.

Cycling enthusiasts will find Italy a welcoming destination, with numerous cycling routes that cater to all levels of experience. From leisurely rides through the Tuscan countryside to challenging mountain trails in the Dolomites, cycling provides an eco-friendly and immersive way to explore Italy's landscapes. Many cities also offer bike-sharing programs, allowing for convenient exploration of urban areas without the need for a personal vehicle.

Ferries are an integral part of transportation in Italy, particularly for those wishing to explore the country's numerous islands and coastal regions. The islands of Sicily and Sardinia are accessible by ferry from mainland ports like Naples and Genoa, offering both passenger and vehicle transport. Additionally, ferries provide connections between smaller islands, such as the Aeolian and Pontine archipelagos, allowing travelers to discover Italy's maritime charm.

Air travel remains a viable option for covering long distances quickly, with a network of domestic flights connecting major cities and regions. Airlines like Alitalia and low-cost carriers such as Ryanair and EasyJet operate numerous routes within Italy, making it possible to traverse the country in a matter of hours. While air travel may lack the scenic allure of other modes of transportation, it offers convenience for those on tight schedules.

Navigating public transportation within Italian cities is generally straightforward, with efficient systems in place to connect key areas. Cities like Rome, Milan, and Naples boast metro networks that facilitate easy access to major attractions and neighborhoods. Buses and trams complement these networks, providing comprehensive coverage throughout urban areas. Purchasing a city pass or transportation card can simplify travel and offer significant savings, particularly for those planning to use public transport frequently.

Taxis and ride-sharing services, such as Uber and Lyft, are available in most cities, offering a convenient option for short distances or when public transportation is less accessible. It's advisable to use official taxi services, as they're regulated and often more reliable. In smaller towns, taxis may be less prevalent, so it's worth arranging for transportation in advance or relying on alternative methods.

When planning your transportation strategy for Italy, consider the nature of your itinerary and personal preferences. Each mode of transport offers distinct advantages, from the efficiency of high-speed trains to the freedom of a rental car. By combining different options, you can tailor your journey to suit your interests and pace, ensuring a well-rounded and enriching travel experience.

Italy's transportation network, with its blend of modernity and tradition, is a testament to the country's dynamic character. By understanding and embracing the various options available, travelers can unlock the full potential of their Italian adventure, creating a journey that is as memorable as it is diverse. Whether you choose to glide along shimmering railways, cruise through winding roads, or sail across azure waters, Italy promises an unforgettable exploration of its many wonders.

2.2. Italian Phrases for Travelers

Mastering a few essential Italian phrases can significantly enhance your travel experience, opening doors to richer interactions and deeper cultural immersion. While many Italians in tourist areas speak English, making an effort to converse in their language can lead to warmer receptions and unexpected rewards. The Italian language is not just a means of communication; it is a vibrant expression of the country's rich heritage and cultural nuances.

Begin with basic greetings, as these set the tone for any interaction. "Buongiorno" (good morning) and "Buonasera" (good evening) are polite ways to greet someone, while "Ciao" serves as a casual hello or goodbye among friends. When meeting someone for the first time, "Piacere" (nice to meet you) is a courteous expression to show your pleasure in the introduction.

Navigating Italy requires some practical language skills, especially when it comes to asking for directions or information. "Dov'è" (where is) followed by the place you're looking for, like "la stazione" (the station) or "il bagno" (the bathroom), will help you find your way. If you're lost, "Mi sono perso" (I am lost) can prompt helpful assistance from locals. To inquire about the time, "Che ore sono?" (what time is it?) is a straightforward question.

Dining in Italy is a cultural experience, and knowing how to communicate in restaurants and cafes can enhance your enjoyment. Upon entering an eatery, a simple "Buonasera, un tavolo per due, per favore" (good evening, a table for two, please) sets the stage for a pleasant meal. When ordering, "Vorrei" (I would like) followed by the dish name shows your intent politely. If you have dietary restrictions, phrases like "Sono allergico a" (I am allergic to) or "Sono vegetariano" (I am vegetarian) can be crucial.

Shopping in Italy offers the chance to practice your language skills in a different context. When browsing, "Quanto costa?" (how much does it cost?) is essential for inquiring about prices. Bargaining is not as common in Italy as in other cultures, but showing interest and politeness can sometimes lead to a better deal. When making a purchase, "Vorrei comprare" (I would like to buy) ensures clarity.

Transportation interactions often involve specific vocabulary. At a train station or airport, "Un biglietto per" (a ticket to) followed by your destination is a practical phrase to remember. If you need to know departure times, "A che ora parte?" (what time does it leave?) will help you plan your journey. When taking a taxi, providing the address with "Mi porti a" (take me to) streamlines communication.

Engaging with locals can lead to some of the most rewarding travel experiences. Italians are generally warm and welcoming, and a few key phrases can deepen these connections. "Parla inglese?" (do you speak English?) is a gentle way to bridge language gaps, while "Mi scusi" (excuse me) is useful for getting someone's attention politely. If someone offers assistance, "Grazie mille" (thank you very much) shows your appreciation.

Understanding common expressions and responses is also beneficial. "Sì" (yes) and "No" (no) are straightforward, but knowing "Forse" (maybe) or "Non lo so" (I don't know) can be useful in various situations. If you need something repeated, "Può ripetere, per favore?" (can you repeat, please?) is a polite request. When expressing regret or an apology, "Mi dispiace" (I'm sorry) conveys sincerity.

Emergency situations, though rare, require specific language skills. Knowing how to ask for help, "Aiuto!" (help!), is vital, as is being able to say "Chiamate un dottore" (call a doctor) if medical assistance is needed. It's also wise to know "Dov'è l'ospedale?" (where is the hospital?) for more serious situations. Keeping a small card with these phrases written down can be helpful in stressful moments.

While this chapter covers many basic phrases, it's important to remember that language is fluid and context-dependent. Listening attentively and observing body language can provide additional clues to understanding and being understood. Italians are known for their expressive communication style, often using gestures to accompany their words, which can be both entertaining and informative for travelers.

Incorporating these Italian phrases into your travel toolkit will not only facilitate smoother interactions but also enrich your cultural experience. Speaking the local language, even at a basic level, demonstrates respect and appreciation for the culture, often leading to more meaningful connections. As you explore Italy, allow these phrases to guide you through a journey filled with discovery, warmth, and unforgettable memories.

2.3. Accommodation Tips

Finding the right accommodation is a crucial part of planning any trip to Italy, setting the stage for a comfortable and memorable experience. The country offers a diverse range of lodging options, from luxurious hotels in bustling cities to quaint agriturismos in the serene countryside. Selecting the perfect place to stay requires careful consideration of your preferences, budget, and itinerary.

Hotels in Italy range from opulent five-star establishments to budget-friendly options, each providing varying levels of comfort and amenities. Luxury hotels, often located in central city areas, offer exquisite services, including gourmet dining, spa facilities, and breathtaking views. These hotels are ideal for travelers seeking indulgence and convenience, with easy access to major attractions. On the other hand, budget hotels and hostels provide affordability and basic comforts, making them suitable for travelers who prioritize exploration over amenities. When booking a hotel, consider its proximity to public transportation and key sights to minimize travel time and maximize your experience.

Bed and breakfasts (B&Bs) offer a more intimate and often personalized lodging experience. These accommodations are typically family-run and provide a homely atmosphere, allowing guests to connect with local culture and hospitality. Staying at a B&B often includes a hearty breakfast featuring regional specialties, offering a delightful start to your day. B&Bs can be found in both urban centers and rural areas, providing flexibility depending on your travel plans. When choosing a B&B, read reviews to ensure the hosts are accommodating and the location aligns with your itinerary.

For those seeking a unique and immersive experience, agriturismos present an excellent opportunity to explore Italy's rural charm. These farm-stay accommodations offer guests the chance to engage with traditional agricultural practices, enjoy homemade meals, and relax in scenic surroundings. Agriturismos are particularly popular in regions like Tuscany and Umbria, where rolling vineyards and olive groves set a picturesque backdrop. Staying at an agriturismo not only supports local farmers but also provides a deeper understanding of Italy's agrarian heritage.

Vacation rentals, such as apartments and villas, provide flexibility and privacy, making them a popular choice for families and groups. Renting an apartment allows you to live like a local, with the freedom to cook your meals and explore neighborhood markets. Villas, often located in idyllic countryside settings, offer spacious accommodations with amenities like private pools and gardens. When considering a vacation rental, ensure the property is equipped with necessary facilities and check for any additional fees, such as cleaning charges or security deposits.

Hostels, known for their affordability and social atmosphere, cater to budget-conscious travelers and backpackers. Many hostels in Italy provide dormitory-style accommodations and communal areas, fostering opportunities to meet fellow travelers. Some hostels also offer private rooms for those seeking more privacy while maintaining a budget-friendly approach. Location is key when selecting a hostel, so choose one that is close to public transport and attractions to make the most of your stay.

Italy's rich history is reflected in its unique lodging options, such as staying in a historic villa or a converted monastery. These accommodations offer a glimpse into the past, with architecture and decor that transport you back in time. Staying in a historic property can add an extra layer of enchantment to your trip, creating lasting memories. When selecting such accommodations, consider their location and amenities, as some may lack modern conveniences.

Booking your accommodation well in advance is advisable, especially during peak travel seasons, such as summer and major holidays. Early booking ensures you have a wider range of options and can often result in better rates. Utilize reputable booking platforms and read reviews to gauge the quality and reliability of potential accommodations. Additionally, consider booking directly through the accommodation's website, as this may offer exclusive deals or perks.

Incorporating local experiences into your stay can enhance your understanding and appreciation of Italian culture. Many accommodations offer activities such as cooking classes, wine tastings, and guided tours, providing an insider's perspective on local traditions and customs. Participating in these activities not only enriches your travel experience but also supports local businesses and communities.

Being mindful of cultural norms and practices while staying in Italy can lead to a more respectful and enjoyable visit. Italians value politeness and courtesy, so greeting hosts with a friendly "buongiorno" or "buonasera" is appreciated. Respecting quiet hours, typically observed in the afternoon and late evening, ensures harmony with your hosts and fellow guests. When staying in rural areas, be aware of local customs, such as mealtime etiquette and dress codes, to avoid misunderstandings.

Consider sustainability when choosing accommodations, as eco-friendly options are increasingly available in Italy. Many hotels and lodgings have adopted green practices, such as using renewable energy, reducing waste, and supporting local ecosystems. By opting for sustainable accommodations, you contribute to the preservation of Italy's natural beauty and cultural heritage for future generations.

Ultimately, the choice of accommodation can greatly influence your Italian adventure. Whether you prefer the opulence of a luxury hotel, the charm of a B&B, the authenticity of an agriturismo, or the freedom of a vacation rental, each option offers unique experiences that cater to different preferences and budgets. By carefully selecting a place to stay that aligns with your travel goals, you set the foundation for an unforgettable journey through Italy's captivating landscapes and vibrant culture.

2.4. Budgeting for Your Trip

Crafting a budget for your Italian journey is a vital step in ensuring a stress-free and enjoyable experience. A well-thought-out financial plan allows you to make the most of your trip without the worry of overspending. From airfare to gelato, understanding the costs associated with travel in Italy and managing your finances effectively can elevate your adventure from ordinary to extraordinary.

Begin by identifying your primary expenses, starting with transportation. Airfare is often the most significant initial cost, and booking in advance can lead to substantial savings. Utilize fare comparison websites and consider flying into less congested airports, such as Pisa or Bologna, where flights may be more affordable than major hubs like Rome or Milan. Monitoring for discounts and being flexible with your travel dates can also help reduce costs.

Once in Italy, transportation expenses continue with local travel. As previously discussed, Italy's train network is both efficient and cost-effective. Purchasing a rail pass can offer savings for those planning to travel extensively by train. For local transportation, consider city passes that offer unlimited travel on buses, trams, and metros, providing both convenience and value. If you opt for car rental, factor in additional costs such as fuel, tolls, and parking fees, which can add up quickly.

Accommodation is another significant component of your travel budget. Italy offers a wide range of lodging options to suit different budgets, from luxury hotels to budget hostels. Determine what level of comfort you desire and allocate funds accordingly. Booking accommodations in advance can secure better rates, especially during peak tourist seasons. Additionally, consider alternative lodging such as vacation rentals or agriturismos, which can provide a more economical and immersive experience.

Dining in Italy is a highlight for many travelers, and budgeting for food requires a balance between indulgence and economy. Sampling Italy's renowned cuisine doesn't have to break the bank. Seek out local trattorias and osterias, where you can enjoy authentic meals at reasonable prices. Street food offers a budget-friendly and delicious alternative, with options like pizza al taglio and panini readily available. Allocate funds for special dining experiences, such as a multi-course meal in a renowned restaurant, while balancing your budget with simpler fare.

Entertainment and activities are integral to experiencing Italy's rich culture and history. Entry fees for museums, galleries, and historical sites can add up, so it's wise to prioritize must-see attractions and explore free or discounted options. Many cities offer museum passes that provide access to multiple sites at a reduced cost. Additionally, outdoor activities such as hiking in the Dolomites or strolling through Tuscany's vineyards offer enriching experiences without significant expense.

Shopping is another consideration for your budget, particularly if you plan to purchase souvenirs or indulge in Italy's fashion offerings. Set a spending limit for shopping and focus on meaningful purchases that reflect your journey. Local markets and artisan shops often offer unique items at reasonable prices, providing authentic mementos of your trip.

Unexpected expenses are an inevitable part of travel, making it essential to set aside a contingency fund. This reserve can cover unforeseen costs such as medical emergencies, last-minute itinerary changes, or incidental purchases. Aim to keep approximately 10-15% of your total budget available for these contingencies, providing peace of mind and financial flexibility.

Currency exchange and payment methods also play a role in your budgeting considerations. While credit cards are widely accepted in urban areas, having cash on hand is advisable for smaller towns or establishments that may not accept card payments. Exchange rates can fluctuate, so monitor them and exchange currency when rates are favorable. Consider using a travel-friendly credit card that offers low foreign transaction fees to maximize your purchasing power.

Travel insurance is a prudent investment that can protect your travel budget from unforeseen disruptions. Policies vary, so select one that covers essentials such as medical emergencies, trip cancellation, and lost luggage. While it may seem like an additional cost, travel insurance can save significant expenses in unexpected situations, ensuring your trip proceeds smoothly.

Budgeting for your Italian adventure requires a comprehensive approach, balancing fixed expenses with discretionary spending. By planning ahead and allocating funds wisely, you can enjoy Italy's diverse offerings without financial strain. Remember, a well-managed budget enhances your travel experience, enabling you to focus on exploration and discovery rather than financial concerns.

Italy's allure lies not only in its landscapes and culture but also in the experiences it offers. By budgeting effectively, you can create a personalized and enriching journey that reflects your interests and priorities. As you wander through Italy's historic streets and picturesque countryside, your thoughtful financial planning will ensure each moment is savored to the fullest, creating cherished memories that last a lifetime.

2.5. Safety and Health Information

Ensuring your safety and well-being while traveling in Italy involves a combination of awareness, preparation, and understanding local customs. This beautiful country offers a plethora of experiences, and with a few practical steps, you can enjoy your journey with peace of mind and confidence.

Traveling in Italy is generally safe, but like any destination, it requires vigilance. Petty crime, such as pickpocketing, is a common concern in crowded areas, particularly in major cities like Rome, Milan, and Naples. To safeguard your belongings, consider using an anti-theft bag and keep valuables like passports and money in a secure, concealed pouch. Staying alert in busy areas, such as train stations and tourist attractions, reduces the risk of theft. Be wary of distractions or scams that aim to divert your attention, and always be cautious when approached by strangers offering unsolicited help.

Health considerations begin before you arrive in Italy. Consult with a healthcare professional regarding any vaccinations or medications you might need, particularly if you have pre-existing health conditions. While Italy does not have specific vaccination requirements for travelers, staying up-to-date on routine vaccinations is advisable. If you require prescription medications, bring an adequate supply and carry a copy of the prescription in case you need to refill it while abroad. It's also wise to research any specific health advisories or potential risks related to the areas you plan to visit.

Access to healthcare in Italy is generally excellent, with a well-established network of hospitals and clinics. EU citizens benefit from the European Health Insurance Card (EHIC), which grants access to public healthcare services at reduced costs. Non-EU travelers should ensure they have comprehensive travel insurance that includes medical coverage. In the event of a medical emergency, knowing key phrases like "Chiamate un'ambulanza" (call an ambulance) or "Dov'è l'ospedale?" (where is the hospital?) can be crucial.

Italy's climate varies significantly from north to south, and being prepared for weather-related conditions is essential for staying healthy. In summer, temperatures can soar, especially in southern regions, so staying hydrated and using sun protection is vital. Conversely, winter in northern Italy can be cold, particularly in mountainous areas, requiring appropriate clothing to prevent hypothermia or frostbite. Checking the weather forecast and packing accordingly ensures comfort and safety throughout your trip.

Adapting to Italian road safety practices is crucial if you plan to drive. Roads can be narrow and winding, especially in rural areas, and local driving styles may differ from what you're accustomed to. Familiarize yourself with Italian traffic laws, such as speed limits and the use of seatbelts, to avoid accidents and fines. If you're renting a car, ensure it is equipped with necessary safety features and that you have an international driving permit if required. For those cycling, wearing a helmet and using designated bike lanes where available enhances safety.

Italy's rich culinary culture is a highlight for many travelers, but it's important to exercise caution with food and water. Tap water is generally safe to drink in Italy, but if you have a sensitive stomach, bottled water is a readily available alternative. When dining, ensure that food is freshly prepared and cooked thoroughly to avoid potential foodborne illnesses. If you have dietary restrictions or allergies, communicate these clearly to restaurant staff to prevent adverse reactions.

Being aware of local laws and customs is part of staying safe and respecting Italian culture. Laws regarding alcohol consumption, smoking, and drug use are strictly enforced, and ignorance is not an excuse. Understanding these regulations helps avoid legal issues and ensures a respectful interaction with locals. Additionally, observing cultural norms, such as dress codes when visiting religious sites, fosters positive relations and enhances your experience.

In light of global health concerns, staying informed about public health guidelines and travel advisories is more important than ever. Monitor updates from reputable sources, such as government health departments or the World Health Organization, for information on any travel restrictions or necessary precautions. Having a flexible itinerary and being prepared for possible changes ensures a smoother experience in uncertain times.

Emergency numbers are crucial to know, with 112 serving as the universal emergency number across Europe, including Italy. This number connects you to police, fire, or medical services, ensuring prompt assistance when needed. Having a charged mobile phone and knowing the location of your nearest embassy or consulate provides additional support in emergencies.

Ultimately, a successful and safe trip to Italy hinges on preparation, awareness, and adaptability. By taking proactive steps to protect your health and safety, you can fully immerse yourself in the beauty and culture that Italy offers. Each region, from the sun-drenched coasts of Sicily to the historic streets of Florence, presents opportunities for discovery and adventure, with your well-being as the foundation for a memorable journey.

2.6. Off-the-Beaten-Path Travel Strategies

Exploring Italy beyond its famed landmarks offers a deeper connection to the country's essence. While the Colosseum and the Leaning Tower of Pisa are iconic, venturing off the beaten path reveals the true heart of Italy, where traditions thrive and authentic encounters await. Crafting a journey that includes lesser-known destinations requires a blend of curiosity, research, and an adventurous spirit.

Begin by considering regions often overlooked by the tourist crowds. The region of Basilicata, for example, is home to Matera, a city renowned for its ancient cave dwellings, the Sassi. This UNESCO World Heritage Site offers a glimpse into Italy's past, where you can wander through winding alleys and explore rock-hewn churches. Another hidden gem is the region of Friuli Venezia Giulia, where the town of Cividale del Friuli enchants visitors with its medieval architecture and rich Celtic history. These destinations offer unique perspectives on Italy's diverse cultural tapestry.

To uncover hidden treasures, immerse yourself in local festivals and traditions that reflect Italy's vibrant heritage. The Infiorata in Spello, Umbria, is a stunning floral festival where streets are transformed into intricate tapestries of petals. Participating in such events not only enriches your experience but also connects you with the community's spirit and customs. Seek out sagre, local food festivals, which celebrate regional specialties, from truffles in Piedmont to artichokes in Lazio. These gatherings provide an opportunity to taste authentic flavors and engage with locals in a festive atmosphere.

Embarking on scenic drives allows you to discover Italy's picturesque countryside and charming villages. The Val d'Orcia in Tuscany offers a landscape of rolling hills, cypress-lined roads, and rustic farmhouses, perfect for a leisurely drive. In Calabria, the Costa degli Dei, or Coast of the Gods, presents breathtaking views of the Tyrrhenian Sea and quaint fishing villages like Pizzo and Tropea. These routes invite you to pause, savor the scenery, and uncover lesser-known spots at your own pace.

Hiking enthusiasts will find Italy's diverse terrain offers ample opportunities for exploration. The Path of the Gods, or Sentiero degli Dei, on the Amalfi Coast is a spectacular trail that winds through dramatic cliffs and offers panoramic vistas of the azure sea below. For a more secluded experience, the Gran Paradiso National Park in the Aosta Valley provides trails through pristine alpine landscapes, where wildlife such as ibex and chamois roam freely. These hikes offer both physical challenge and spiritual reward, connecting you with nature's beauty and serenity.

Staying in agriturismos or rural accommodations not only supports local farmers but also provides an authentic taste of Italian life. These farm stays offer a chance to participate in activities such as olive oil production, wine tasting, or cooking classes, providing insight into regional practices and culinary traditions. By choosing to stay in these accommodations, you immerse yourself in the rhythms of rural life, gaining a deeper appreciation for Italy's agricultural heritage.

Engaging with local artisans and craftspeople unveils Italy's rich artistic traditions, often overshadowed by mass-produced souvenirs. Visit workshops in cities like Florence or Venice to observe craftsmen at work, creating everything from intricate lace to exquisite glassware. In the town of Deruta, renowned for its ceramics, you can witness artisans painting vibrant patterns on pottery, a skill passed down through generations. Purchasing directly from these artisans not only supports their craft but also ensures you take home a unique piece of Italy.

Exploring Italy's coastline by boat offers a fresh perspective on its natural beauty. The Pontine Islands, a volcanic archipelago off the coast of Lazio, boast crystal-clear waters and secluded beaches, accessible by ferry or private boat. In Liguria, the Cinque Terre's rugged cliffs and colorful villages are best appreciated from the sea, where you can discover hidden coves and swim in the Mediterranean's turquoise depths. These aquatic adventures provide a sense of freedom and discovery, revealing facets of Italy often missed from the land.

To navigate these off-the-beaten-path adventures, flexibility and adaptability are key. Embrace the unexpected, whether it's a chance encounter with a local or a spontaneous detour to explore a curious landmark. Allow time in your itinerary for serendipitous discoveries, as these often become the most memorable moments of your journey. Equip yourself with a reliable map or travel app, as some remote areas may have limited connectivity, and be prepared for varying road conditions in rural regions.

Learning a few basic Italian phrases enhances your interactions and fosters goodwill with locals. While English is spoken in many tourist areas, using Italian demonstrates respect and appreciation for the culture. Simple greetings, expressions of gratitude, and questions about directions or recommendations can lead to enriching exchanges and insider tips.

As you venture beyond the familiar, remember that travel is as much about the journey as the destination. Italy's hidden corners offer tales of history, culture, and nature waiting to be discovered. By stepping off the beaten path, you engage with Italy on a deeper level, creating experiences that resonate long after your return. Each encounter, be it with a landscape, a festival, or a local, adds a unique thread to the tapestry of your Italian adventure, weaving a story that is entirely your own.

3. HIDDEN GEMS OF NORTHERN ITALY

3.1. Undiscovered Treasures of Venice

Venice, often celebrated for its iconic canals and grand architecture, harbors a wealth of undiscovered treasures that lie beyond the well-trodden paths of St. Mark's Square and the Rialto Bridge. For those willing to delve deeper into this enchanting city, Venice offers hidden gems that reveal its rich tapestry of history, culture, and everyday life.

Begin your exploration by venturing into the sestieri, or districts, less frequented by tourists. Cannaregio, one of the city's largest districts, offers a glimpse into authentic Venetian life. Here, you'll find the Jewish Ghetto, a historic enclave dating back to the 16th century. Stroll through its quiet streets and discover synagogues and kosher bakeries that preserve the traditions of Venice's Jewish community. The Museo Ebraico provides insight into this rich cultural heritage, with exhibits that chronicle the history and customs of the ghetto's residents.

In Cannaregio, the Fondamenta della Misericordia is a picturesque canal-side promenade lined with charming cafes and local eateries. Enjoy a leisurely aperitivo while watching the world go by, or indulge in a cicchetti crawl, sampling Venetian tapas in a series of bacari. This authentic dining experience allows you to savor local flavors and engage with Venetians in a relaxed setting.

Dorsoduro, another sestiere, is home to a thriving arts scene and offers a different perspective on Venetian culture. The Peggy Guggenheim Collection, housed in a former palazzo on the Grand Canal, showcases an impressive array of modern art, from Picasso to Pollock. This museum provides a striking contrast to the city's Renaissance and Baroque masterpieces, highlighting Venice's role as a hub of artistic innovation.

In Dorsoduro, explore the Fondazione Vedova, dedicated to the works of Emilio Vedova, a key figure in Italian abstract expressionism. This dynamic space hosts rotating exhibitions and events that celebrate contemporary art. Nearby, the quiet streets and canals of the Zattere offer a peaceful escape, with stunning views of the Giudecca Island and the Venetian Lagoon.

The island of Giudecca itself is a hidden gem, often overlooked by visitors focused on the main island. Accessible by vaporetto, this tranquil retreat offers a respite from the city's bustling center. Visit the Chiesa del Redentore, a masterpiece of Palladian architecture, known for its stunning façade and serene interior. Each July, the Festa del Redentore celebrates the church's completion with a spectacular fireworks display over the lagoon, a tradition cherished by Venetians.

The Orto Botanico, Venice's botanical garden, is a lesser-known oasis in the San Marco district. Established by the University of Padua, this garden boasts a diverse collection of plants and serves as a center for research and conservation. Wander its pathways and discover rare species, enjoying the tranquility and beauty of this hidden sanctuary.

For a unique perspective on Venice's maritime heritage, visit the Arsenale, the historic shipyard that was once the heart of the Venetian Republic's naval power. Though parts of the Arsenale are restricted, guided tours offer insights into its storied past and the innovations that propelled Venice to maritime supremacy. The nearby Museo Storico Navale delves deeper into this legacy, with exhibits showcasing naval artifacts and models.

Venice's islands offer further opportunities for discovery. The island of Burano, famous for its lace-making tradition, is a kaleidoscope of color, with its brightly painted houses lining the canals. Wander through this lively community and observe artisans at work, preserving the delicate craft of lace-making. Nearby, the island of Torcello offers a step back in time, with its ancient cathedral and Byzantine mosaics evoking the early days of the Venetian lagoon's settlement.

One of Venice's most intriguing secrets lies beneath its surface. The city's network of subterranean canals and tunnels, known as the "sottoportego," offers a hidden world waiting to be explored. Guided tours provide access to these enigmatic passages, revealing a side of Venice few have seen. Discover the engineering marvels that have sustained the city for centuries, gaining a deeper appreciation for its resilience and ingenuity.

Engaging with Venice's lesser-known cultural institutions enriches your understanding of its multifaceted identity. The Ca' Pesaro International Gallery of Modern Art, housed in a grand Baroque palace, presents an eclectic collection of 19th and 20th-century works. From Klimt to Kandinsky, the museum offers a journey through diverse artistic movements, complemented by temporary exhibitions that showcase emerging talent.

To truly connect with Venice's soul, embrace the slower pace and immerse yourself in the rhythm of local life. Attend a classical concert in one of the city's opulent churches, where the strains of Vivaldi or Monteverdi transport you to another era. Participate in a mask-making workshop, learning the intricate art of crafting the iconic Venetian masks that symbolize the city's storied past. These experiences foster a deeper connection with Venice, transcending the superficial allure of its famous sights.

Navigating Venice's labyrinthine streets requires a spirit of curiosity and a willingness to get lost. Allow yourself to wander without a fixed itinerary, discovering hidden squares, quaint bridges, and quiet corners that reveal the city's true character. Engage with locals, who often share insights and stories that enrich your journey, offering glimpses into the everyday life of this extraordinary city.

As you uncover Venice's undiscovered treasures, you'll find a city that defies cliché and exceeds expectations. Beyond the gondolas and grand palaces, Venice reveals itself as a living, breathing entity, where history and modernity coexist in a delicate balance. Each hidden gem adds a new dimension to your understanding, weaving a tapestry of experiences that linger long after your return. Through these encounters, Venice becomes more than a destination; it becomes a part of your own story, a chapter of discovery and wonder that unfolds with each step you take.

3.2. Lake Como's Secret Spots

Nestled amid the majestic Italian Alps, Lake Como is renowned for its opulent villas and serene waters. However, beyond its well-trodden paths lies a treasure trove of hidden spots waiting to be discovered by those willing to venture off the beaten track. These secret locations offer a glimpse into the authentic charm and tranquility that define this enchanting region.

Start your exploration in the charming village of Nesso, a place often overshadowed by its more famous neighbors. Here, the Cascata di Nesso, a stunning waterfall, cascades dramatically into a gorge. The ancient Ponte della Civera, a stone bridge spanning the gorge, offers breathtaking views of the waterfall and the lake beyond. This picturesque setting, coupled with the village's narrow streets and traditional houses, provides a perfect escape from the hustle and bustle of more crowded areas.

A short ferry ride from the bustling town of Bellagio lies the island of Comacina, steeped in history and legend. Once a fortified stronghold, the island now offers a serene retreat with its lush greenery and ancient ruins. Wander its paths and discover the remnants of early Christian churches, whispering the stories of a bygone era. The island's only restaurant, Locanda dell'Isola Comacina, promises a unique dining experience with a menu that has remained unchanged for decades, complemented by the enchanting ritual of the "fire coffee."

The village of Varenna, often overlooked in favor of Bellagio or Menaggio, boasts a wealth of hidden gems. The Villa Monastero, once a Cistercian convent, enchants visitors with its exquisite gardens and eclectic architecture. Stroll along the lakefront promenade, the Passeggiata degli Innamorati, where stunning vistas of the lake and surrounding mountains unfold at every turn. Varenna's quiet charm and timeless beauty make it a perfect place to unwind and absorb the essence of Lake Como.

For those seeking solitude, the Sentiero del Viandante, or Path of the Wanderer, offers an idyllic hiking experience. This ancient trail, running along the eastern shore of Lake Como, reveals panoramic views and untouched landscapes. As you traverse the path, you'll encounter quaint hamlets and terraced vineyards, each with its own story to tell. The journey invites introspection and connection with nature, far removed from the throngs of tourists.

In the shadow of Monte Legnone lies the village of Dervio, a haven for outdoor enthusiasts. With its unspoiled beaches and well-equipped marina, Dervio beckons those who wish to sail or windsurf on the lake's shimmering waters. Inland, the surrounding hills offer trails for hiking and cycling, providing sweeping views of the lake and distant peaks. The village's relaxed pace and welcoming atmosphere make it a delightful base for exploring Lake Como's natural splendor.

The sleepy village of Pognana Lario, perched on the lake's western shore, offers a glimpse into traditional life in the region. Here, the ancient church of San Miro, with its frescoes and Romanesque architecture, stands as a testament to the area's rich history. The village's quiet streets and family-run trattorias invite visitors to slow down and savor the simple pleasures of life by the lake.

Further south, the town of Torno captivates with its cobbled streets and historic architecture. The medieval Church of San Giovanni Battista, with its intricate frescoes, is a highlight, offering insight into the town's artistic heritage. A short hike leads to the Sentee di Sort, a panoramic trail that rewards with breathtaking views of the lake and the surrounding mountains. Torno's peaceful ambiance and stunning vistas make it a hidden gem worth discovering.

Exploring Lake Como's lesser-known spots also means embracing its culinary traditions. In the village of Bellano, the local specialty of misultin, sun-dried lake fish, offers a taste of the region's rich gastronomic heritage. Pair this delicacy with polenta, a staple of Lombard cuisine, for an authentic dining experience. The region's restaurants and osterias, often family-run, provide a warm welcome and a chance to savor the flavors of Lake Como.

Venturing to the northern reaches of the lake, the village of Gravedona surprises with its blend of history and natural beauty. The majestic Church of Santa Maria del Tiglio, a masterpiece of Romanesque architecture, stands by the lakeside, offering a serene spot for reflection. The nearby Parco Valle Albano invites visitors to explore its lush landscapes and discover the diverse flora and fauna that flourish in this protected area.

For a unique perspective on Lake Como, take to the water on a traditional Lucia boat. These small wooden vessels, once used by fishermen, offer an intimate way to explore the lake's hidden coves and secluded beaches. Guided tours provide fascinating insights into the lake's ecology and history, revealing stories of the people who have called this enchanting place home for centuries.

Ultimately, discovering Lake Como's secret spots is about embracing the spirit of adventure and curiosity. As you wander its shores and delve into its hidden corners, you'll uncover a world of beauty and wonder that extends beyond the surface. Each hidden gem adds depth to your understanding of this captivating region, creating memories that linger long after your journey ends. Through these experiences, Lake Como reveals its true essence, a tapestry of history, nature, and culture woven together in a harmonious embrace.

3.3. Turin: Italy's Underrated Gem

Turin, often overshadowed by Italy's more celebrated cities, is a hidden gem that offers a rich tapestry of history, culture, and innovation. Situated in the shadow of the Alps, this northern city boasts a unique blend of architectural grandeur, culinary excellence, and artistic heritage that provides a captivating experience for those who venture to explore its streets.

Begin your journey in the heart of Turin at Piazza Castello, a sprawling square that reflects the city's royal past. Dominated by the Palazzo Madama and the Palazzo Reale, this area serves as a testament to Turin's status as the former capital of the Kingdom of Sardinia. The Palazzo Reale, with its opulent rooms and expansive gardens, offers a glimpse into the lives of the Savoy dynasty. A guided tour reveals exquisite frescoes and collections of art and armory, immersing you in the regal history that shaped the region.

Adjacent to the royal palace stands the Turin Cathedral, home to the enigmatic Shroud of Turin. While the shroud itself is rarely on display, the cathedral's solemn beauty and the accompanying museum provide insight into this relic's significance and the ongoing debates surrounding its authenticity. This spiritual and historical landmark invites contemplation and reflection, adding a layer of mystery to Turin's allure.

For art enthusiasts, the Museo Egizio is a must-visit destination. Renowned as one of the most significant collections of Egyptian antiquities outside Cairo, the museum showcases artifacts that span millennia. From intricately painted sarcophagi to monumental statues, the exhibits transport visitors to the land of the pharaohs, offering an educational and awe-inspiring experience. The museum's dedication to research and preservation underscores Turin's commitment to cultural heritage.

As you wander through Turin's elegant boulevards, the city's architectural diversity becomes evident. The Mole Antonelliana, an iconic symbol of Turin, towers over the cityscape. Originally conceived as a synagogue, this striking structure now houses the National Museum of Cinema. A panoramic elevator ride to the top offers breathtaking views of the city and the surrounding Alps, while the museum itself provides an engaging exploration of the history of film, complete with interactive exhibits and vintage memorabilia.

Turin's culinary scene is another facet of its charm, blending traditional Piedmontese flavors with contemporary innovation. The historic Caffè Torino invites you to savor a bicerin, a decadent concoction of espresso, chocolate, and cream that has been a local favorite for centuries. For a taste of Turin's renowned chocolate, visit one of the city's artisanal chocolatiers, where you can sample gianduiotti, creamy hazelnut-infused confections that melt in your mouth.

The bustling Mercato di Porta Palazzo, one of Europe's largest open-air markets, offers a sensory feast. Here, vendors display an array of fresh produce, cheeses, and cured meats, reflecting the region's agricultural bounty. Stroll through the market's vibrant stalls and engage with local artisans and food purveyors, discovering the ingredients that form the backbone of Piedmontese cuisine.

For those with a penchant for innovation and design, Turin's automotive heritage is showcased at the Museo Nazionale dell'Automobile. This museum traces the evolution of the automobile, with exhibits ranging from early prototypes to futuristic concept cars. As the birthplace of Fiat, Turin has played a pivotal role in shaping the automotive industry, and the museum's collection highlights this legacy with creativity and style.

The Quadrilatero Romano, Turin's historic center, invites exploration with its narrow cobblestone streets and hidden courtyards. This vibrant neighborhood comes alive in the evening, with its array of trattorias, wine bars, and boutiques offering a taste of the city's nightlife. Enjoy a leisurely aperitivo, a beloved Italian tradition, as you soak in the atmosphere and engage with locals who call this charming district home.

Turin's commitment to contemporary art is evident in venues like the Fondazione Sandretto Re Rebaudengo, a dynamic space dedicated to promoting emerging artists. With its ever-changing exhibitions and thought-provoking installations, the foundation serves as a platform for dialogue and creativity, reflecting Turin's innovative spirit. Similarly, the Castello di Rivoli, a short distance from the city, houses an impressive collection of contemporary art within the walls of a historic palace, offering a striking juxtaposition of past and present.

Nature enthusiasts will find solace in Turin's green spaces, such as the Parco del Valentino. This expansive park, nestled along the banks of the Po River, provides a tranquil escape with its botanical gardens, walking trails, and the charming Borgo Medievale, a reconstructed medieval village. Whether you're picnicking on the grass or rowing a boat on the river, the park offers a serene retreat from urban life.

Throughout the year, Turin hosts a variety of festivals and events that highlight its cultural diversity and artistic prowess. The Torino Film Festival, one of Italy's most prestigious cinematic events, attracts filmmakers and cinephiles from around the world, while the Salone del Gusto celebrates the region's culinary heritage with tastings, workshops, and discussions led by renowned chefs and food experts.

Turin's public transportation system, including trams and buses, makes it easy to navigate the city and explore its many attractions. For a more personal experience, consider renting a bicycle to traverse the city's bike-friendly paths, allowing you to discover hidden corners and local gems at your own pace.

Embracing Turin's underrated charm involves a willingness to delve beneath the surface and engage with the city's multifaceted identity. From its royal history and architectural wonders to its culinary delights and contemporary art scene, Turin offers a rich tapestry of experiences that captivate and inspire. As you uncover the layers of this vibrant city, you'll find that Turin is not just a destination, but a revelation, inviting you to explore, engage, and embrace its unique spirit.

3.4. The Dolomites: Beyond the Ski Resorts

The Dolomites, a majestic mountain range in northeastern Italy, are renowned for their striking peaks and world-class ski resorts. Yet, beyond the bustling winter activities lies a landscape teeming with hidden wonders and year-round attractions that offer a unique perspective on this UNESCO World Heritage site. Exploring the Dolomites beyond the ski slopes unveils a realm of natural beauty, cultural richness, and outdoor adventures that captivate the soul.

Start your journey in the charming town of Cortina d'Ampezzo, often referred to as the "Queen of the Dolomites." While its winter sports facilities are celebrated, Cortina offers a wealth of experiences during the warmer months as well. The town's vibrant atmosphere, set against the backdrop of towering peaks, provides a perfect base for exploring the surrounding area. Wander through its picturesque streets, where boutiques, cafes, and local artisans display the region's craftsmanship and hospitality.

Venture into the heart of the Dolomites, where the Tre Cime di Lavaredo, or Three Peaks, stand as iconic symbols of the region. These three towering rock formations offer breathtaking vistas and are a haven for hikers and climbers alike. Trails of varying difficulty levels wind through alpine meadows and rugged terrain, each turn revealing panoramic views that inspire awe and reflection. For those less inclined to hike, the nearby Misurina Lake offers a serene setting for a leisurely stroll or a peaceful paddle.

The Dolomites' unique geology and biodiversity make them a paradise for nature enthusiasts. The Parco Naturale Paneveggio-Pale di San Martino, a protected area within the Dolomites, is home to diverse flora and fauna. Explore its lush forests and discover the harmonious balance between nature and conservation. The park's visitor center provides insights into the region's natural history and the efforts to preserve its delicate ecosystems.

Cultural exploration in the Dolomites reveals a tapestry of traditions and influences. The Ladin people, an ethnic minority in the region, offer a glimpse into a unique cultural heritage that has been preserved over centuries. Villages such as Ortisei and San Cassiano celebrate Ladin language, crafts, and cuisine. Engage with local artisans, who create intricate wood carvings and textiles that reflect the Ladin identity. Sampling traditional Ladin dishes, such as canederli (bread dumplings) or speck (smoked ham), offers a taste of the region's culinary diversity.

For a deeper connection to the Dolomites' history, visit the Messner Mountain Museum, a series of museums dedicated to mountain culture and the legacy of famed mountaineer Reinhold Messner. Each museum, located in strategic sites throughout the Dolomites, offers a unique perspective on the relationship between humans and the mountains. From exhibits on the history of alpinism to the spiritual significance of mountains in various cultures, the museums provide an enriching exploration of the region's past and present.

Cycling enthusiasts will find the Dolomites a thrilling playground, with its winding roads and challenging climbs. The Sellaronda, a circular route that loops around the Sella massif, offers cyclists a scenic and exhilarating ride. Whether tackling the route independently or joining a guided tour, the experience promises breathtaking views and a sense of accomplishment. For those seeking more leisurely rides, the Dolomites' extensive network of bike trails caters to all skill levels, allowing you to explore the landscape at your own pace.

In the quaint village of Bolzano, the South Tyrol Museum of Archaeology houses one of the region's most intriguing discoveries: Ötzi the Iceman. This naturally mummified corpse, dating back over 5,000 years, provides a fascinating glimpse into prehistoric life in the Alps. The museum's exhibits unravel the mystery of Ötzi's life and death, offering insights into the tools, clothing, and nutrition of a bygone era. Bolzano's blend of Italian and Austrian influences is reflected in its architecture, cuisine, and language, creating a unique cultural fusion that enriches the visitor experience.

The Dolomites' thermal springs offer a relaxing reprieve for weary travelers. Resorts such as the Terme di Comano or the Terme di Merano provide rejuvenating spa treatments and natural thermal waters set against the stunning mountain backdrop. These wellness centers harness the healing properties of the mineral-rich waters, promoting relaxation and well-being amidst the tranquility of the alpine environment.

Throughout the year, the Dolomites host a variety of festivals and events that celebrate their cultural and natural heritage. The Dolomiti Balloon Festival in January fills the skies with vibrant hot air balloons, offering a unique perspective on the snow-covered landscape. In summer, the Alta Badia region hosts the Maratona dles Dolomites, a prestigious cycling marathon that attracts participants from around the world. These events provide opportunities to engage with local communities and experience the Dolomites' lively spirit.

Accommodation options in the Dolomites range from cozy mountain huts to luxurious resorts, each offering a distinct experience of the region's hospitality. Staying in a rifugio, or mountain hut, allows you to immerse yourself in the alpine environment, with rustic accommodations and hearty meals that nourish both body and soul. For a touch of elegance, boutique hotels and chalets offer modern amenities and stunning views, providing a comfortable retreat after a day of exploration.

Navigating the Dolomites' diverse landscape requires a spirit of adventure and a willingness to embrace the unexpected. Whether you're hiking a remote trail, savoring a Ladin feast, or simply soaking in the beauty of the mountains, the Dolomites invite you to connect with nature and culture in profound ways. Each hidden nook and craggy peak tells a story of resilience and wonder, creating a mosaic of experiences that enrich your journey.

As you uncover the Dolomites beyond the ski resorts, you'll find a region that defies expectations and captivates the imagination. The mountains, with their timeless allure and myriad secrets, offer a sanctuary for exploration and reflection. Through these encounters, the Dolomites become more than a destination; they become an integral part of your personal narrative, a testament to the enduring beauty and mystery of nature.

3.5. Emilia-Romagna's Culinary Secrets

In the heart of Italy lies Emilia-Romagna, a region renowned for its gastronomic excellence and culinary traditions that have captivated palates worldwide. This fertile land, stretching from the Apennines to the Po River, is a veritable cornucopia of flavors, where the art of food extends beyond mere sustenance to become a celebration of culture and identity. Delving into Emilia-Romagna's culinary secrets unveils a world of artisanal craftsmanship, time-honored recipes, and vibrant local markets that define this culinary haven.

Begin your culinary journey in Bologna, often hailed as the gastronomic capital of Italy. Known affectionately as "La Grassa" or "The Fat," Bologna is a city where food is revered and savored. The city's narrow streets are lined with trattorias and osterias offering traditional dishes that showcase the region's bounty. The iconic tagliatelle al ragù, often mistakenly referred to as spaghetti Bolognese outside Italy, is a must-try. This dish features silky ribbons of fresh pasta coated in a rich, slow-cooked meat sauce, a testament to the Bolognese dedication to culinary perfection. To truly appreciate the art of pasta-making, consider taking a cooking class where local chefs impart the secrets of crafting the perfect pasta dough and achieving the ideal sauce consistency.

Parma, another gem in Emilia-Romagna, is synonymous with two of Italy's most celebrated products: Parmigiano-Reggiano cheese and Prosciutto di Parma. These artisanal delicacies are the result of centuries-old traditions and strict production standards that ensure their unparalleled quality. A visit to a Parmigiano-Reggiano dairy offers insight into the meticulous process of cheese-making, from the careful selection of milk to the aging of wheels in temperature-controlled rooms. Tasting the cheese at various stages of maturation reveals its evolving flavors and textures, from nutty and crumbly to rich and complex.

In the nearby town of Langhirano, the air is fragrant with the scent of curing hams. Here, the production of Prosciutto di Parma is a labor of love, where pork legs are salted and aged in the region's unique microclimate. A guided tour of a prosciutto cellar unveils the delicate balance of temperature and humidity that transforms the meat into a savory masterpiece, celebrated for its melt-in-the-mouth tenderness and sweet, nutty flavor. Savoring thin slices of Prosciutto di Parma, paired with a glass of Lambrusco, encapsulates the essence of Emilia-Romagna's culinary heritage.

Venturing to Modena, one encounters the exquisite tradition of Aceto Balsamico Tradizionale, or traditional balsamic vinegar. Unlike the commercial balsamic vinegar found in supermarkets, this artisanal product is crafted from the must of local grapes, cooked down and aged for a minimum of 12 years in a series of wooden barrels. The result is a dark, syrupy vinegar with a complex bouquet of sweet and tangy notes. Visiting an acetaia, or vinegar producer, provides an opportunity to learn about the intricate aging process and to taste this liquid gold, often served sparingly over Parmigiano-Reggiano or strawberries.

The fertile plains of Emilia-Romagna are dotted with vibrant markets that celebrate the region's agricultural abundance. In the city of Ferrara, the bustling Mercato Coperto is a feast for the senses, where stalls brim with seasonal produce, fresh seafood, and artisanal breads. Engaging with local vendors offers insights into the region's culinary traditions, as they share stories of heirloom varieties and time-honored recipes passed down through generations. Sampling the local specialty of cappellacci di zucca, pumpkin-filled pasta served with sage and butter, provides a taste of Ferrara's unique flavors.

Emilia-Romagna's culinary secrets extend beyond its iconic products to embrace a diverse array of regional specialties. In the town of Piacenza, the dish of pisarei e faso, small dumplings served with a hearty bean and tomato sauce, reflects the region's rustic roots. Meanwhile, in the coastal town of Rimini, the piadina, a thin flatbread filled with an array of ingredients from cured meats to fresh vegetables, offers a quick and satisfying meal that captures the essence of Italian street food.

For those seeking a deeper connection to the land, agritourism offers an immersive experience in Emilia-Romagna's agricultural heartland. Farm stays provide an opportunity to participate in the rhythms of rural life, from harvesting grapes and olives to foraging for wild truffles. These experiences foster a deeper appreciation for the region's culinary heritage and the dedication of the farmers and artisans who sustain it.

Wine enthusiasts will find much to explore in Emilia-Romagna's diverse vineyards, where a variety of indigenous grape varieties thrive. The sparkling red Lambrusco, often misunderstood outside Italy, is a revelation when tasted in its homeland. With its refreshing acidity and fruity notes, it pairs beautifully with the region's rich cuisine. In the hills surrounding Bologna, the white wine Pignoletto offers a crisp and floral contrast to the hearty dishes of the region.

Throughout Emilia-Romagna, festivals and events celebrate the region's culinary traditions, offering visitors a chance to engage with local communities and experience the vibrancy of Italian culture. The Fiera di San Donnino in Fidenza, for example, is a lively event where local producers showcase their artisanal goods, from cheeses and cured meats to wines and pastries. These gatherings provide a window into the region's culinary soul, where food is not just sustenance but a way of life.

As you delve into Emilia-Romagna's culinary secrets, you'll discover a region where the art of food is woven into the fabric of everyday life. From the bustling markets and artisanal producers to the rustic trattorias and elegant osterias, each encounter offers a taste of the region's rich culinary heritage. Through these experiences, Emilia-Romagna reveals itself as a land of abundance and tradition, where the love of food and the joy of sharing it are celebrated with every meal. The culinary journey through this enchanting region is a feast for the senses, a celebration of flavors and aromas that linger long after the last bite.

3.6. Cinque Terre: Away from the Crowds

The allure of Cinque Terre, with its picturesque villages perched on rugged cliffs overlooking the Ligurian Sea, has captivated travelers for decades. Yet, the popularity of this UNESCO World Heritage site often leads to bustling crowds, particularly during peak tourist seasons. To truly appreciate the charm and tranquility of this coastal paradise, one must seek out the hidden corners and lesser-known paths that offer a more intimate experience of the region's beauty.

Begin your exploration in the village of Corniglia, the middle gem among the five lands, and the only one not directly adjacent to the sea. Its elevated position on a rocky promontory provides sweeping views of the azure waters and vineyards below. Accessible by a steep staircase known as the Lardarina or a shuttle bus, Corniglia's narrow streets and pastel-colored houses exude an air of tranquility. Wander through its alleyways, where the scent of lemon trees and the sound of church bells create a serene atmosphere far removed from the bustling waterfronts of its neighboring villages.

From Corniglia, venture onto the Sentiero Azzurro, a network of hiking trails that connects the five villages. While the entire trail offers breathtaking vistas, certain sections are less traveled, providing a sense of solitude and connection with nature. The stretch between Corniglia and Vernazza, for example, meanders through terraced vineyards and olive groves, offering glimpses of the sea through the foliage. As you walk, the rhythmic lapping of waves and the rustle of leaves compose a natural symphony that accompanies you on your journey.

For a truly secluded experience, consider exploring the lesser-known trails that lead away from the main path. The hike to the Santuario di Nostra Signora di Montenero, perched high above Riomaggiore, rewards with panoramic views and a peaceful sanctuary away from the crowds. The ascent, though challenging, offers a rewarding escape into the verdant hills, where wildflowers and butterflies add splashes of color to the landscape.

In the village of Manarola, escape the tourist throngs by venturing to the Punta Bonfiglio, a scenic promontory that offers unobstructed views of the coastline. Here, a small bar serves refreshing beverages, inviting you to pause and savor the moment. As the sun dips below the horizon, the sky is set ablaze with hues of orange and pink, casting a warm glow over the village's vibrant facades.

The Cinque Terre region is also home to a series of sanctuaries, each with its own unique charm and historical significance. The Santuario della Madonna di Reggio, located above Vernazza, is a tranquil retreat surrounded by chestnut trees and offering a respite from the bustling village below. The sanctuary's peaceful ambiance invites reflection and contemplation, and the views from its terrace reveal a stunning panorama of the coastline and the distant Ligurian mountains.

For those seeking a culinary adventure, the local cuisine of Cinque Terre offers a taste of the region's rich heritage. Away from the crowded restaurants, you'll find family-run trattorias and osterias where traditional recipes are lovingly prepared. Savor a plate of trofie al pesto, a pasta dish that showcases the region's famed basil pesto, or indulge in a serving of anchovies, freshly caught and marinated in olive oil and lemon. Pair your meal with a glass of Sciacchetrà, a sweet dessert wine produced from the region's sun-drenched vineyards.

The village of Monterosso al Mare, known for its sandy beaches and vibrant atmosphere, also harbors quiet corners for those who seek them. Venture to the quieter Fegina Beach, where the golden sands and crystalline waters invite relaxation and rejuvenation. Nearby, the Capuchin Monastery offers a peaceful haven with its shaded gardens and panoramic views of the coastline. The monastery's simple beauty and serene surroundings make it an ideal spot for meditation and introspection.

As the sun sets over the Ligurian Sea, the magic of Cinque Terre truly comes alive. The villages, illuminated by the warm glow of street lamps, take on an ethereal quality as the night sky fills with stars. Wander through the quiet streets, where the sound of laughter and the clinking of glasses spill from open windows, and the aroma of freshly baked focaccia lingers in the air. These moments, away from the hustle and bustle, reveal the authentic spirit of Cinque Terre—a place where time seems to stand still and the beauty of nature and human craftsmanship converge in perfect harmony.

For a unique perspective on Cinque Terre, take to the water and explore the coastline by boat. Small, locally operated tours offer an intimate experience, allowing you to discover hidden coves and secluded beaches that are inaccessible by land. The gentle rocking of the boat and the sound of the waves create a soothing rhythm as you glide along the coast, offering a new appreciation for the rugged beauty of the cliffs and the vibrant colors of the villages.

In the off-season, when the crowds have thinned and the pace of life slows, Cinque Terre reveals a different facet of its charm. The mild climate and quiet streets invite leisurely exploration, and the sense of community among the locals becomes more pronounced. Engage with the residents, who are often eager to share stories of their heritage and traditions, and gain a deeper understanding of the region's unique identity.

Ultimately, discovering Cinque Terre away from the crowds involves embracing the slower pace and hidden treasures that define this enchanting region. Whether you're hiking a solitary trail, savoring a meal in a quiet trattoria, or simply watching the sunset from a secluded vantage point, these moments of tranquility and connection offer a glimpse into the soul of Cinque Terre. As you uncover its secrets, you'll find that the true magic of this coastal paradise lies not in the well-trodden paths, but in the quiet corners and untold stories that await the curious traveler.

3.7. Lesser-Known Tuscan Villages

Amidst the rolling hills and golden landscapes of Tuscany lie hidden treasures often overshadowed by the region's iconic cities. These lesser-known villages offer glimpses into authentic Tuscan life, where tradition and tranquility reign supreme. Each village, with its unique charm and history, invites exploration beyond the well-trodden paths, promising experiences rich with culture, gastronomy, and breathtaking scenery.

Begin your Tuscan adventure in the quaint village of San Quirico d'Orcia, nestled in the heart of the Val d'Orcia. This medieval gem, with its well-preserved architecture and ancient city walls, offers a step back in time. Stroll through its cobblestone streets, where stone buildings adorned with colorful flowers create a picturesque setting. The Collegiata di San Quirico, a Romanesque church with intricate carvings, stands as a testament to the village's historical significance. Nearby, the Horti Leonini gardens, a beautifully manicured space dating back to the Renaissance, provide a peaceful retreat and a panoramic view of the surrounding countryside.

Journeying north, the village of Montemerano awaits, perched on a hilltop amidst vineyards and olive groves. This small village, part of the Maremma region, exudes a sense of timelessness with its narrow alleyways and rustic charm. The Piazza del Castello, the village's central square, is surrounded by ancient stone buildings that echo with stories of the past. In Montemerano, the fusion of art and history is evident in the Chiesa di San Giorgio, where frescoes and artworks tell tales of devotion and artistry. As the sun sets, the village takes on a magical glow, with the warm hues of its stone walls casting a spell over all who wander its paths.

Venture to the less-visited village of Suvereto, known for its medieval heritage and robust wines. This small but vibrant community, nestled in the hills of the Etruscan Coast, is enveloped by lush landscapes and vineyards. Suvereto's ancient streets and fortified walls transport visitors to a bygone era, while its local vineyards offer tastings of rich reds and crisp whites, reflecting the region's winemaking prowess. The village's culinary scene is a celebration of traditional Tuscan flavors, with restaurants serving dishes crafted from local ingredients, including wild boar and fresh pasta.

In the heart of the Chianti region lies the village of Radda in Chianti, a quintessential Tuscan settlement surrounded by rolling vineyards and verdant hills. Known for its excellent wines, Radda is a haven for oenophiles seeking to explore the complexities of Chianti Classico. Wine cellars and enotecas line the village streets, offering tastings and insights into the winemaking process. Beyond wine, Radda's charm is found in its historic center, where ancient churches and quaint shops offer a glimpse into village life. The surrounding countryside beckons with trails perfect for hiking and cycling, allowing visitors to immerse themselves in nature's tranquility.

Moving eastward, the village of Anghiari captivates with its medieval architecture and dramatic setting atop a hill overlooking the Tiber Valley. Known for the Battle of Anghiari, famously depicted by Leonardo da Vinci, this village is steeped in history. Its narrow streets and stone houses tell stories of resilience and artistic heritage. The Museo della Battaglia di Anghiari offers a deeper understanding of the village's historical significance, showcasing artifacts and exhibits that bring the past to life. Anghiari's artisans continue to uphold the village's creative legacy, producing handcrafted goods and traditional textiles that reflect the region's cultural richness.

For those seeking a coastal escape, the village of Castiglione della Pescaia offers a blend of history and seaside charm. This picturesque fishing village, with its medieval fortress and sandy beaches, provides a tranquil retreat along the Tyrrhenian Sea. Castiglione's vibrant marina buzzes with activity, offering opportunities for sailing and exploring the nearby islands. The village's culinary offerings celebrate the bounty of the sea, with restaurants serving fresh seafood dishes that highlight the region's coastal flavors.

As you traverse these lesser-known Tuscan villages, the essence of Tuscany reveals itself in the simplicity and authenticity of village life. Each settlement, with its unique character and heritage, offers a window into the soul of the region—a place where time-honored traditions and natural beauty coexist in harmony. The warmth of the local people, the rustic charm of the architecture, and the breathtaking landscapes create an unforgettable tapestry that invites exploration and reflection.

The journey through these hidden gems of Tuscany is a celebration of discovery and connection. Whether savoring a glass of wine in a Chianti vineyard, wandering through the medieval streets of Anghiari, or gazing at the sunset over the Val d'Orcia, each moment encapsulates the timeless allure of Tuscany. These lesser-known villages, with their stories and secrets, offer a profound sense of place, where the past and present intertwine to create a rich and enduring legacy. As you explore these enchanting locales, you become part of the tapestry of Tuscany, a region that continues to inspire and captivate all who venture into its embrace.

4. CENTRAL ITALY'S AUTHENTIC EXPERIENCES

4.1. Rome: Beyond the Colosseum

Rome, the Eternal City, is synonymous with iconic landmarks like the Colosseum, the Vatican, and the Pantheon. Yet, beyond these well-trodden paths lies a treasure trove of lesser-known wonders that offer a more intimate glimpse into the city's rich tapestry of history, art, and culture. To truly experience Rome's multifaceted charm, one must venture off the beaten track, exploring its hidden gems and savoring the essence of Roman life.

Begin your exploration in the vibrant neighborhood of Trastevere, a district that effortlessly combines old-world charm with a bohemian spirit. Its narrow, cobblestone streets are lined with ivy-clad buildings, quaint cafes, and artisan shops. Here, the Basilica di Santa Maria in Trastevere, one of the oldest churches in Rome, awaits with its stunning mosaics and serene ambiance. As you wander through Trastevere, the lively piazzas come alive with the sounds of street musicians and the aroma of Roman cuisine wafts from trattorias serving traditional dishes like cacio e pepe and supplì.

Crossing the Tiber River, the Aventine Hill beckons with its lush gardens and panoramic vistas. This quiet residential area offers a respite from the city's bustling pace, with attractions that reveal Rome's hidden depths. The Giardino degli Aranci, or Orange Garden, is a peaceful oasis where visitors can enjoy spectacular views of the city skyline, framed by fragrant orange trees. Nearby, the keyhole of the Knights of Malta provides a whimsical peek at the dome of St. Peter's Basilica, perfectly framed by the garden's hedges—a secret delight that captivates both locals and visitors alike.

For art enthusiasts, the Galleria Borghese houses a remarkable collection of masterpieces within the opulent Villa Borghese. Nestled amidst the sprawling gardens of the Borghese estate, the gallery boasts works by Caravaggio, Bernini, and Raphael, offering a feast for the eyes in an intimate setting. A leisurely stroll through the surrounding gardens reveals tranquil fountains, manicured lawns, and hidden sculptures, inviting reflection and appreciation of Rome's artistic legacy.

The Testaccio neighborhood, once the hub of ancient Rome's port, is a testament to the city's dynamic evolution. Today, it stands as a vibrant cultural district known for its culinary delights and contemporary art scene. The Testaccio Market, a bustling hub of local produce and street food, offers a taste of authentic Roman life. Here, you can sample fresh mozzarella, porchetta, and artisanal gelato, immersing yourself in the flavors that define Roman cuisine. The neighborhood is also home to the MACRO Testaccio, a contemporary art museum housed in a former slaughterhouse, showcasing cutting-edge exhibitions that reflect Rome's modern artistic sensibilities.

In the heart of the city, the Jewish Ghetto reveals a rich tapestry of history and tradition. As one of the oldest Jewish communities in Europe, this area is steeped in cultural significance. The Great Synagogue of Rome, with its stunning architecture and museum, offers insights into the Jewish experience in Rome throughout the centuries. The ghetto's narrow streets are lined with kosher bakeries and restaurants, where you can savor traditional dishes like carciofi alla giudia, a crispy fried artichoke that exemplifies the fusion of Jewish and Roman culinary influences.

For those seeking a deeper connection to Rome's ancient past, the Appian Way, or Via Appia Antica, offers a journey through history. This ancient road, once a vital artery of the Roman Empire, is now a peaceful escape from the city's hustle and bustle. As you walk or cycle along its cobblestones, you'll encounter ancient tombs, catacombs, and ruins that whisper tales of Rome's storied past. The serene landscape, dotted with cypress trees and rolling hills, provides a contemplative setting for reflection and exploration.

In the lesser-known district of Garbatella, a unique architectural experiment from the early 20th century unfolds. Designed as a garden suburb, Garbatella's winding streets and colorful buildings create a charming atmosphere that feels worlds away from the city's grandeur. The neighborhood's vibrant community life is evident in its lively squares and local markets, where the spirit of Roman hospitality shines through. Exploring Garbatella offers a glimpse into the everyday life of Romans, away from the tourist crowds.

The Baths of Caracalla, though overshadowed by Rome's more famous ruins, are a testament to the grandeur of the ancient Roman Empire. These sprawling thermal baths, once a center of social and recreational life, now serve as a hauntingly beautiful reminder of Rome's architectural prowess. Strolling through the remains of the vaulted halls and mosaic floors, one can almost hear the echoes of the past reverberating through the stone.

As night falls, Rome's vibrant nightlife offers a different perspective on the city's allure. The Monti neighborhood, with its eclectic mix of bars, vintage shops, and trattorias, comes alive with energy and creativity. Whether sipping an aperitivo at a rooftop bar or dancing to live music in a hidden speakeasy, the spirit of Rome is palpable in the laughter and camaraderie that fill the air.

4.2. Florence's Artisan Workshops

Florence, the cradle of the Renaissance, is a city where art and craftsmanship are woven into the very fabric of its identity. Beyond the grandeur of its cathedrals and museums lies a hidden world of artisan workshops, where centuries-old techniques are preserved and celebrated. These ateliers, tucked away in the city's narrow streets and bustling squares, offer a glimpse into the heart of Florentine culture and the dedication of its craftsmen.

Start your journey in the Oltrarno district, the beating heart of Florence's artisan community. Crossing the Ponte Vecchio, the bustling bridge lined with jewelry shops, leads you to a neighborhood rich in history and creativity. Here, the spirit of craftsmanship thrives in workshops that have stood the test of time. Each studio presents a unique opportunity to witness the meticulous process of creating art by hand, from leather goods and jewelry to textiles and paper.

At the heart of the Oltrarno is the Santo Spirito square, a vibrant area where artisans have honed their skills for generations. Among them, the leatherworkers of Florence are renowned for their exquisite craftsmanship. Step into a workshop where the scent of tanned hides fills the air and skilled hands cut, stitch, and emboss leather into objects of beauty and utility. From handbags and wallets to belts and shoes, each piece reflects a commitment to quality and tradition.

Observing the artisans at work reveals the intricate techniques passed down through generations, ensuring that each creation is a true work of art.

Nearby, the art of jewelry-making shines brightly in Florence's goldsmith workshops. The tradition of crafting fine jewelry dates back to the Renaissance, when master goldsmiths created stunning pieces for the Medici family. Today, you can watch as artisans meticulously shape precious metals and set gemstones, transforming raw materials into stunning adornments. In these intimate studios, the clinking of tools and the focused concentration of the craftsmen create an atmosphere of creativity and dedication.

Florence's rich history of textile production is celebrated in the workshops of weavers and embroiderers who continue to craft exquisite fabrics by hand. Visit a weaving studio where looms clatter rhythmically, producing intricate patterns and textures that tell stories of the past. The skillful interplay of threads and colors results in textiles that are as much a joy to behold as they are to touch. In embroidery ateliers, delicate needlework brings to life motifs inspired by the city's artistic heritage, from floral designs to intricate monograms.

The art of bookbinding and paper marbling is another cherished tradition in Florence's artisan landscape. In small workshops, craftsmen transform sheets of paper into beautifully bound journals and albums, each adorned with marbled covers that swirl with vibrant hues. The process of marbling, where colors dance across a liquid surface before being transferred to paper, is mesmerizing to witness. These artisans, with their steady hands and keen eyes, ensure that each book is a testament to the enduring beauty of handmade craftsmanship.

Florence's artisans are not only guardians of tradition but also innovators who infuse contemporary flair into their creations. In the city's ateliers, you'll find artists experimenting with new techniques and materials, pushing the boundaries of their craft while remaining rooted in heritage. This blend of tradition and innovation is evident in the work of ceramicists who create modern interpretations of classic Florentine motifs. Their pieces, with their bold colors and dynamic forms, reflect a city that embraces both its past and its future.

As you explore Florence's artisan workshops, you'll encounter craftsmen eager to share their passion and expertise. Many studios offer workshops and classes, inviting visitors to try their hand at traditional techniques and experience the joy of creating something with their own hands. Whether it's crafting a piece of jewelry, binding a book, or painting a ceramic tile, these experiences provide a deeper connection to the art and culture of Florence.

The dedication of Florence's artisans is evident not only in their work but also in their commitment to preserving the city's cultural heritage. Organizations and associations support these craftsmen, ensuring that their skills are passed on to future generations. Initiatives such as apprenticeships and collaborative projects foster a sense of community among artisans, allowing them to share knowledge and inspire one another.

Throughout your journey, the stories of these craftsmen and women add depth to the experience. You'll hear tales of families who have practiced their craft for centuries, of artisans who have mastered their skills through years of practice, and of newcomers who bring fresh perspectives to traditional techniques. These narratives, woven into the fabric of Florence, reveal a city that celebrates the artistry of its people and the enduring legacy of its craft.

Florence's artisan workshops offer more than just beautiful objects; they provide a window into the soul of the city. Each piece, lovingly crafted by skilled hands, tells a story of passion, dedication, and creativity. As you wander through the streets of Florence, from the bustling markets to the quiet studios, you'll discover a world where craftsmanship is not just a skill but a way of life. The legacy of Florence's artisans is one of resilience and innovation, a testament to the power of creativity to shape and define a city.

In the end, the true beauty of Florence lies not only in its monuments and museums but in the spirit of its people—the artisans who continue to breathe life into ancient traditions while embracing the possibilities of the future. Their work, a harmonious blend of past and present, is a reminder of the enduring power of art to inspire and transform. As you leave Florence, the memories of its workshops and the warmth of its artisans will linger, a testament to the city's timeless allure and the magic of its craftsmanship.

4.3. Umbria: The Green Heart of Italy

Nestled in the heart of Italy, Umbria is a region that captivates with its verdant landscapes, rich history, and vibrant culture. Often overshadowed by its more famous neighbor Tuscany, Umbria offers a tranquil escape into the essence of Italian life. Its rolling hills, medieval hill towns, and lush valleys create an idyllic setting that beckons travelers seeking to explore the country's authentic soul.

Umbria's landscape is a tapestry of green, earning it the moniker "The Green Heart of Italy." The region's natural beauty is best appreciated in its abundant national parks and nature reserves. One such gem is the Monti Sibillini National Park, where the Apennine Mountains rise majestically, offering a haven for hikers and nature enthusiasts. Trails weave through dense forests and alpine meadows, leading to panoramic vistas that stretch as far as the eye can see. In spring and summer, the park bursts into a riot of colors with wildflowers carpeting the hillsides, creating a stunning mosaic against the backdrop of rugged peaks.

The charm of Umbria lies not only in its landscapes but also in its picturesque villages that seem to have been plucked straight from a storybook. Perched on hilltops, these medieval towns are steeped in history and tradition. One such village is Spello, renowned for its ancient walls and Roman architecture. As you wander through its narrow streets, adorned with vibrant flower boxes and medieval arches, the sense of history is palpable. Spello is also famous for its Infiorate di Spello, a festival where intricate floral carpets are created to celebrate Corpus Christi, turning the village into a kaleidoscope of colors and scents.

Another must-visit town is Assisi, the birthplace of St. Francis, whose legacy permeates the town's spiritual and cultural fabric. The Basilica di San Francesco, a UNESCO World Heritage site, is a masterpiece of medieval art and architecture, housing frescoes by renowned artists such as Giotto and Cimabue. As you explore Assisi, the peaceful ambiance and stunning views of the surrounding countryside provide a sense of serenity and reflection.

In the heart of Umbria lies the city of Perugia, the region's capital and a vibrant hub of culture and history. Perugia's medieval center is a labyrinth of cobblestone streets, lively piazzas, and historic buildings. The city's rich artistic heritage is showcased in the Galleria Nazionale dell'Umbria, home to works by artists like Perugino and Pinturicchio. Perugia is also famous for its annual Umbria Jazz Festival, which attracts world-renowned musicians and jazz enthusiasts from around the globe, transforming the city into a lively celebration of music and culture.

Umbria's culinary traditions are a testament to the region's agricultural abundance and commitment to quality ingredients. The fertile valleys yield an array of produce, from olives and grapes to truffles and legumes. The town of Norcia, known for its black truffles and cured meats, offers a taste of Umbria's gastronomic excellence. Here, the art of butchery is celebrated, with local shops showcasing an array of sausages, salami, and prosciutto. A visit to Norcia is incomplete without savoring a dish of strangozzi al tartufo, a pasta dish that highlights the earthy flavors of the region's prized truffles.

Wine enthusiasts will find delight in Umbria's vineyards, where the rolling hills produce a variety of wines that reflect the region's unique terroir. The area around Montefalco is renowned for its Sagrantino wine, a bold and robust red that has gained international acclaim. Visiting the vineyards and wineries offers an opportunity to learn about the winemaking process and sample the rich flavors that define Umbrian wines.

Umbria's spiritual and artistic legacy is also evident in its numerous abbeys, monasteries, and sanctuaries that dot the landscape. The Abbey of Monte Oliveto Maggiore, set amidst olive groves and cypress trees, is a place of quiet contemplation and architectural beauty. Its frescoed cloisters and serene surroundings provide a glimpse into the monastic life that has shaped the region's cultural identity.

The town of Orvieto, perched atop a volcanic plateau, boasts a remarkable cathedral that stands as a testament to Umbria's artistic heritage. The Duomo di Orvieto, with its intricate façade and stunning frescoes, is a masterpiece of Gothic architecture and a symbol of the town's historical significance. The underground city of Orvieto, with its network of Etruscan caves and tunnels, offers a fascinating journey into the past, revealing the ingenuity and resilience of its ancient inhabitants.

As you explore Umbria, the warmth and hospitality of its people add to the region's allure. The Umbrians' deep connection to their land and traditions is evident in their festivals, markets, and daily life. Whether sharing a meal at a family-run trattoria or participating in a local celebration, you'll find a genuine sense of community and pride that enriches the experience of visiting this enchanting region.

Umbria's beauty lies in its ability to embrace the past while welcoming the present, offering a harmonious blend of history, nature, and culture. From the rolling hills and serene valleys to the vibrant towns and villages, Umbria invites you to slow down and savor the simple pleasures of life. As you journey through the Green Heart of Italy, you'll discover a region that captivates the senses and nourishes the soul, leaving you with memories that linger long after you've departed its verdant embrace.

4.4. Le Marche: Italy's Best-Kept Secret

Le Marche, a region nestled between the Adriatic Sea and the Apennine Mountains, remains a hidden treasure in Italy's diverse landscape. Often overshadowed by its more famous neighbors, Tuscany and Umbria, this enchanting region offers an authentic slice of Italian life, with its unspoiled countryside, charming medieval towns, and a coastline that sparkles under the Mediterranean sun. Le Marche invites exploration, revealing its secrets to those willing to venture beyond the usual tourist trails.

Begin your journey in Urbino, a Renaissance gem that stands as a testament to the region's rich cultural heritage. The town's historic center, a UNESCO World Heritage site, is dominated by the majestic Palazzo Ducale, home to the National Gallery of the Marche. Within its walls, masterpieces by artists such as Piero della Francesca and Raphael, who was born here, captivate with their beauty and craftsmanship. Wandering through the cobblestone streets of Urbino, you can sense the artistic spirit that has shaped this town, from its elegant architecture to its vibrant student life, thanks to the prestigious University of Urbino.

Heading east, the Adriatic Coast beckons with its golden sandy beaches and charming seaside towns. Senigallia, with its velvet beach and lively summer festivals, offers a perfect blend of relaxation and entertainment. The town's historic center, with its elegant piazzas and the imposing Rocca Roveresca fortress, invites exploration and leisurely strolls. Further south, the Conero Riviera boasts dramatic cliffs and crystal-clear waters, where hidden coves and secluded beaches provide a serene escape from the hustle and bustle of modern life.

Le Marche's allure extends beyond its coastal beauty to its picturesque hilltop towns, each with its unique character and history. Ascoli Piceno, known for its stunning Piazza del Popolo, is a jewel of medieval architecture. The square's harmonious design, surrounded by elegant arcades and historic buildings, creates a sense of timelessness. Sipping a coffee at one of the cafes while observing the daily rhythms of life, you feel immersed in the town's rich heritage and vibrant atmosphere.

The Sibillini Mountains, part of the Apennines, offer a different kind of adventure, attracting nature lovers and outdoor enthusiasts. This national park, with its rugged peaks and lush meadows, is a haven for hikers and cyclists. Trails lead through ancient forests and past alpine lakes, providing breathtaking views at every turn. In spring, the Piano Grande, a vast plateau at the foot of the mountains, bursts into a spectacular bloom of wildflowers, creating a tapestry of colors that delights the senses.

Le Marche's culinary traditions are a reflection of its diverse landscape and cultural influences. The region is a paradise for food lovers, with its emphasis on fresh, local ingredients and traditional recipes. The town of Jesi, renowned for its Verdicchio wine, offers a taste of Le Marche's viticultural excellence. This crisp, white wine pairs beautifully with the region's seafood dishes, such as brodetto, a flavorful fish stew that embodies the essence of the Adriatic. Inland, the cuisine takes on a heartier character, with dishes like vincisgrassi, a rich lasagna layered with meat ragù and béchamel, showcasing the region's love for robust flavors.

The town of Macerata, with its open-air Sferisterio arena, is a cultural hub that hosts the annual Macerata Opera Festival, drawing music lovers from around the world. This unique venue, with its impressive acoustics and historic charm, provides a stunning backdrop for performances that celebrate the region's artistic heritage. As the sun sets and the music fills the air, the magic of Le Marche comes alive, offering an unforgettable experience that resonates with the soul.

Le Marche's artisans continue to uphold the region's traditions, producing handcrafted goods that reflect centuries-old skills. In the town of Fabriano, the art of papermaking has flourished since the 13th century, earning it a reputation as the "City of Paper." Visiting the Museo della Carta e della Filigrana offers insight into this ancient craft, with displays of watermarked paper and demonstrations of traditional techniques. The region's commitment to preserving its cultural heritage is evident in the dedication of its craftsmen, who ensure that these skills are passed down through generations.

As you explore the region, the warmth and hospitality of the Marchigiani people add to the charm of your journey. Whether you're dining in a family-run trattoria, tasting olive oil at a local frantoio, or participating in a village festival, you'll find a genuine sense of community and pride in their cultural heritage. This connection to the land and its traditions is palpable, enriching your experience and providing a deeper understanding of what makes Le Marche so special.

Le Marche is a region of contrasts, where the gentle lapping of the Adriatic meets the rugged grandeur of the Apennines, and where ancient towns whisper tales of history amid the bustle of modern life. Its beauty lies in its authenticity and diversity, offering a rich tapestry of experiences that captivate the heart and soul. As you uncover the secrets of this enchanting region, you'll find that Le Marche is more than just a destination; it's a journey into the heart of Italy, where the spirit of discovery and connection thrives.

In the end, Le Marche's magic is found not only in its landscapes and landmarks but in the stories and traditions that define it. The region invites you to slow down, savor each moment, and become part of its living history. As you depart, the memories of its beauty and the warmth of its people will linger, a testament to the enduring allure of Italy's best-kept secret.

4.5. Abruzzo's Wild Beauty

Abruzzo, a region often overlooked in the Italian landscape, is a land where nature reigns supreme. Its wild beauty captivates those who venture into its rugged terrain, offering a profound sense of escape and discovery. From the soaring peaks of the Apennines to the rolling hills and unspoiled coastline, Abruzzo presents a diverse tapestry of natural wonders and authentic experiences that beckon exploration.

The crown jewel of Abruzzo's natural heritage is the Gran Sasso e Monti della Laga National Park, a vast expanse dominated by the majestic Gran Sasso massif. This park is a paradise for outdoor enthusiasts, offering a myriad of opportunities for hiking, climbing, and wildlife watching. The Corno Grande, the highest peak in the Apennines, rises to an impressive 2,912 meters, challenging climbers and rewarding them with panoramic views that stretch across the region. The park's diverse ecosystems support a rich variety of flora and fauna, including the rare Apennine wolf and the Abruzzo chamois, making it a haven for nature lovers and photographers.

Nestled within the park is Campo Imperatore, a high-altitude plateau often referred to as "Little Tibet" for its stark, otherworldly landscapes. Here, the vast open spaces and dramatic skies create a sense of awe and solitude, inviting introspection and connection with nature. The area is dotted with rustic shepherds' huts and grazing livestock, offering a glimpse into the traditional pastoral life that has shaped Abruzzo's cultural identity.

Abruzzo's commitment to conservation is evident in its network of protected areas, which preserve the region's unique biodiversity and landscapes. The Majella National Park, known as the "Mother Mountain," is another gem, characterized by its rugged limestone peaks and deep valleys. The park is home to a wealth of archaeological sites and ancient hermitages, where monks once sought solace and spiritual enlightenment. Exploring these remote sanctuaries, often carved into the rock face, provides a fascinating insight into the region's spiritual heritage and the resilience of its people.

The Sirente-Velino Regional Park, with its dramatic cliffs and hidden caves, offers a different kind of adventure. The park's trails lead through dense forests and past ancient ruins, revealing the stories of the people who have called this land home for millennia. The presence of Neolithic rock carvings and medieval fortresses speaks to the enduring connection between Abruzzo's inhabitants and their rugged environment.

Beyond its mountainous heart, Abruzzo's beauty extends to its picturesque hilltop towns and villages, each with its own unique character and charm. L'Aquila, the region's capital, is a city of resilience, having rebuilt itself after the devastating earthquake of 2009. Its historic center, with its elegant palazzi and vibrant piazzas, reflects the spirit of renewal and determination that defines Abruzzo. The city's rich cultural heritage is celebrated in its museums and festivals, offering a window into the traditions that continue to shape the region.

The medieval village of Santo Stefano di Sessanio, perched high in the Apennines, captivates with its timeless beauty and sense of tranquility. Restored with care, its stone houses and narrow alleys transport visitors back in time, offering a serene escape from the modern world. Nearby, the Rocca Calascio, a striking mountaintop fortress, offers breathtaking views and a sense of adventure for those willing to make the climb.

Abruzzo's coastline, with its pristine beaches and charming fishing villages, provides yet another facet of the region's allure. The Trabocchi Coast, named for its distinctive fishing platforms, is a testament to the region's maritime heritage. These wooden structures, ingeniously designed to catch fish without the need for boats, dot the shoreline and offer a unique dining experience, with many converted into seafood restaurants serving the freshest catch of the day.

The town of Vasto, with its panoramic views of the Adriatic Sea, combines history and natural beauty in equal measure. Its historic center, with its medieval castle and elegant gardens, invites exploration, while the nearby Punta Aderci Nature Reserve offers unspoiled beaches and crystal-clear waters that beckon swimmers and sunbathers alike.

Abruzzo's culinary traditions are deeply rooted in its land and sea, offering a feast of flavors that reflect the region's diverse landscapes. The cuisine is characterized by its simplicity and emphasis on fresh, local ingredients. Arrosticini, skewers of succulent grilled lamb, are a beloved staple, enjoyed at festivals and gatherings throughout the region. The fertile valleys produce an abundance of fruits and vegetables, while the mountains yield prized ingredients like saffron and truffles.

The region's wines, particularly Montepulciano d'Abruzzo and Trebbiano d'Abruzzo, are celebrated for their quality and character, capturing the essence of Abruzzo's terroir. Visiting the vineyards and wineries provides an opportunity to taste these wines and learn about the region's winemaking traditions, which have been passed down through generations.

As you explore Abruzzo, the warmth and hospitality of its people leave a lasting impression. The Abruzzesi are deeply connected to their land and traditions, welcoming visitors with open arms and a genuine desire to share their heritage. Whether you're sharing a meal in a family-run trattoria or participating in a local festival, you'll experience the sense of community and pride that defines this remarkable region.

In Abruzzo, nature and culture intertwine to create a landscape of breathtaking beauty and rich heritage. The region's wild heart beats with a sense of adventure and discovery, inviting you to explore its hidden corners and uncover its secrets. As you journey through Abruzzo, you'll find a place where time seems to stand still, where the beauty of the natural world and the warmth of its people create an unforgettable experience that stays with you long after you've left its rugged embrace.

4.6. Authentic Farmstays and Agriturismos

Immersed in the heart of Italy's vibrant countryside, authentic farmstays and agriturismos offer a retreat from the hustle and bustle of modern life. These rural escapes provide travelers with a unique opportunity to experience Italy's agricultural heritage and savor genuine hospitality. With rustic charm and an intimate connection to nature, agriturismos embody the quintessential Italian lifestyle, inviting guests to embrace simplicity and authenticity.

The concept of agriturismo in Italy is rooted in the tradition of sustainable farming and hospitality. Farmers opened their homes to visitors, sharing their way of life and offering accommodations in a working agricultural environment. This model not only provided farmers with an additional income stream but also fostered a deeper appreciation for rural culture. Today, agriturismos range from simple farmhouses to luxurious estates, each offering a distinctive taste of Italian rural life.

The beauty of staying at an agriturismo lies in the immersive experience it offers. Guests are invited to participate in the daily rhythms of farm life, from harvesting olives and grapes to feeding animals and tending gardens. This hands-on involvement creates a meaningful connection to the land and its produce, allowing visitors to understand the dedication and passion that underpin sustainable farming practices.

Dining at an agriturismo is a feast for the senses, where farm-to-table takes on new meaning. Meals are prepared with fresh, seasonal ingredients sourced directly from the land. The simplicity and quality of the dishes reflect the region's culinary traditions, with flavors that are both comforting and exquisite. Homemade pastas, garden-fresh vegetables, and locally sourced meats are often accompanied by house-made wines and olive oils, creating a culinary experience that is as authentic as it is delicious.

Beyond the daily activities and culinary delights, agriturismos offer a gateway to Italy's picturesque landscapes. Nestled in rolling hills, lush valleys, and verdant vineyards, these farmstays provide stunning backdrops for relaxation and exploration. Whether it's a leisurely stroll through olive groves, a bike ride along country lanes, or simply unwinding with a glass of wine on a sun-drenched terrace, the natural beauty of the surroundings enhances the overall experience.

Each region of Italy offers its own unique agriturismo experience, shaped by local traditions and landscapes. In Tuscany, for instance, guests might find themselves in a farmhouse overlooking vineyards and sunflower fields, with the opportunity to learn about the art of winemaking. In the rolling hills of Umbria, an agriturismo may focus on producing organic olive oil, inviting guests to participate in the harvest and taste freshly pressed oils. In Sicily, visitors might discover the vibrant flavors of citrus fruits and almonds, while in the northern regions, cheese-making and truffle hunting may be highlights of the stay.

Agriturismos also play a crucial role in preserving cultural heritage and supporting local communities. By choosing to stay at these family-run establishments, travelers contribute to the sustainability of rural areas, helping to maintain traditional practices and safeguard the environment. This form of tourism fosters a deeper understanding of the interconnectedness between people, land, and culture, offering a more mindful and responsible way to explore Italy.

For those seeking a truly authentic experience, agriturismos offer a range of activities and workshops that enrich the stay. Cooking classes, for example, provide an opportunity to learn the secrets of Italian cuisine from skilled home cooks, using ingredients sourced directly from the farm. Wine tastings and vineyard tours offer insights into the winemaking process, from grape to glass. Artisanal workshops, such as pottery or cheese-making, allow guests to engage with local crafts and take home a piece of their Italian adventure.

The accommodations at agriturismos vary widely, catering to different tastes and preferences. Some offer rustic charm, with simple, cozy rooms that reflect the farmhouse's history, while others provide modern amenities and luxurious comforts. Regardless of the style, the emphasis is always on creating a warm, welcoming atmosphere where guests feel at home.

Choosing the right agriturismo involves considering factors such as location, activities offered, and the type of experience desired. Whether it's a secluded retreat in the countryside or a vibrant farm close to cultural attractions, there's an agriturismo to suit every traveler. Researching options and reading reviews can provide valuable insights into what each property offers, ensuring a stay that aligns with personal interests and expectations.

One of the most rewarding aspects of staying at an agriturismo is the chance to connect with the hosts and learn about their way of life. These interactions often lead to lasting friendships and cherished memories, as guests are welcomed into the heart of Italian hospitality. Sharing stories over a meal, participating in farm activities, or simply enjoying a quiet moment together fosters a sense of belonging and community.

Agriturismos offer a rare opportunity to slow down and savor the simple pleasures of life. They remind us of the importance of preserving traditions, respecting the land, and nurturing connections with one another. As you leave the farm, the lessons learned and the experiences shared linger, offering a new perspective on life and a deeper appreciation for the beauty of Italy's rural landscapes.

For those seeking a deeper connection to Italy's cultural and natural heritage, agrotourism provides a unique and meaningful way to explore the country's diverse landscapes and traditions. It offers a chance to step off the beaten path, embrace the slower pace of rural life, and discover the true essence of Italy, one farmstay at a time.

5. SOUTHERN ITALY AND ISLANDS UNVEILED

5.1. Naples: Hidden Alleys and Underground Cities

Naples, a city where history and modernity intertwine with palpable vibrancy, offers a labyrinth of hidden alleys and subterranean mysteries that beckon the curious traveler. Its streets, steeped in centuries of culture and tradition, are alive with the echoes of past civilizations. Beneath the bustling surface lies an intricate network of underground passages, revealing a side of Naples that is both captivating and enigmatic.

The city's hidden alleys, or "vicoli," form a maze of narrow, winding streets that pulse with life and character. As you wander through these alleys, the air is filled with the aroma of freshly baked pizzas and the chatter of locals engaged in lively conversation. Each corner unveils a new discovery, from vibrant street art to quaint artisan shops where craftsmen continue age-old traditions. The alleys are a testament to the resilience and creativity of Neapolitans, offering an authentic glimpse into the daily life of this dynamic city.

In the heart of Naples, the Spaccanapoli cuts a straight line through the historic center, an ancient street that embodies the city's soul. Flanked by towering buildings that seem to lean in as if to share secrets, this thoroughfare is a sensory delight. Here, the past mingles with the present, where medieval churches stand alongside bustling markets and modern boutiques. The Basilica di Santa Chiara, with its serene cloister, offers a peaceful respite from the vibrant energy of the streets, inviting reflection amidst the hustle and bustle.

Beneath the surface, Naples' underground world tells a story of resilience and adaptation. The Naples Underground, or Napoli Sotterranea, is an extensive network of tunnels and chambers that date back to ancient times. Originally carved by the Greeks as quarries, these passages were later expanded by the Romans, who used them as aqueducts to supply the city with water. During World War II, the underground served as a refuge for Neapolitans seeking shelter from bombings, providing a sanctuary in times of peril.

Exploring this subterranean realm is a journey into the heart of Naples' history. Guided tours reveal a world where ancient cisterns, catacombs, and hidden chapels coexist, each with its own story to tell. The Catacombs of San Gennaro, for instance, offer a glimpse into early Christian burial practices, with frescoes and mosaics that speak of faith and devotion. The tunnels beneath San Lorenzo Maggiore, meanwhile, uncover layers of the city's past, from Roman markets to medieval streets, illustrating Naples' evolution over millennia.

In the Quartieri Spagnoli, the Spanish Quarter, the spirit of Naples is palpable. This densely populated area is a microcosm of the city's energy, where life spills out onto the streets. Laundry flutters overhead, children play soccer in the alleys, and the sounds of scooters and laughter fill the air. Amidst this vibrant chaos, the quarter's hidden gems await discovery. The Church of Santa Maria degli Angeli alle Croci, with its stunning frescoes and quiet elegance, offers a moment of tranquility amidst the lively surroundings.

The charm of Naples lies in its ability to surprise and delight, with each alley and underground chamber revealing a new facet of the city's character. From the haunting beauty of the Fontanelle Cemetery, an ossuary filled with thousands of skulls, to the lively atmosphere of the Pignasecca market, where vendors peddle everything from fresh produce to vintage treasures, Naples invites exploration and curiosity.

Food, too, is an integral part of the Neapolitan experience, and the city's culinary delights are as diverse as its streets. In the alleys, the aroma of espresso mingles with the scent of sfogliatella, a sweet pastry that embodies the flavors of Naples. Pizzerias, often tucked away in narrow lanes, serve up slices of pizza that have achieved legendary status, their thin crusts and rich toppings a testament to the city's culinary prowess.

The underground wine cellars, carved into the tuff rock, offer a taste of Naples' viticultural heritage. Here, local wines, such as Falanghina and Aglianico, are aged to perfection, capturing the essence of the volcanic soil and the Mediterranean sun. Wine tastings provide an opportunity to savor these flavors, accompanied by tales of the region's winemaking traditions.

Throughout Naples, the past and present coexist in a harmonious dance, inviting visitors to delve deeper into the city's rich tapestry. The hidden alleys and underground cities offer a journey into the heart of Naples, revealing its spirit and resilience. As you navigate these spaces, the stories of those who have walked these paths before echo in the air, a reminder of the enduring legacy of this remarkable city.

In Naples, each step uncovers a new chapter of history, a fresh burst of flavor, a glimpse into the soul of a city that has captivated hearts for centuries. The hidden alleys and underground cities are more than just passages of stone and earth; they are gateways to understanding the essence of Naples, a city that thrives on its ability to embrace the past while forging a future full of promise and possibility.

5.2. Puglia's Trulli and Masserie

Puglia, the sun-drenched heel of Italy's boot, is a region rich in history and architectural wonders. Among its most distinctive features are the trulli and masserie, structures that tell the story of Puglia's past while offering a glimpse into its vibrant present. These iconic buildings, with their unique designs and historical significance, provide an enchanting backdrop to the region's lush landscapes and cultural heritage.

The trulli of Puglia, with their conical roofs and whitewashed walls, are emblematic of the Itria Valley. These whimsical stone dwellings dot the countryside like scattered fairy-tale homes, captivating visitors with their charm and simplicity. Built without mortar, the trulli are a testament to the ingenuity of their creators, who relied on local limestone and ancient construction techniques. The thick stone walls provide natural insulation, keeping the interiors cool in the summer and warm in the winter, a perfect adaptation to the region's climate.

Alberobello, a UNESCO World Heritage site, is the epicenter of trulli architecture. This picturesque town boasts a concentration of over 1,500 trulli, creating a mesmerizing landscape of conical shapes and cobblestone streets. Wandering through Alberobello is like stepping into another world, where time seems to stand still. Each trullo tells a story, from the humble abodes of farmers to the larger, more elaborate structures that served as communal gathering places. The town is a living museum, preserving the traditions and craftsmanship that have defined the region for centuries.

Beyond Alberobello, the Itria Valley offers a tapestry of landscapes where trulli are interwoven with olive groves and vineyards. The countryside is dotted with these charming structures, each with its own history and purpose. Many trulli have been lovingly restored and converted into accommodations, offering visitors a unique opportunity to experience life within these historic walls. Staying in a trullo is a journey into the heart of Puglian culture, where the rustic charm of the past meets the comforts of modern living.

As you venture further into Puglia, the masserie come into view, standing as grand testaments to the region's agricultural heritage. These fortified farmhouses, often surrounded by expansive fields and ancient olive trees, were once the centers of agricultural estates. Built to withstand the threat of invaders, masserie were designed with thick walls and defensive features, providing refuge and security to those who lived and worked within their confines.

Today, many masserie have been transformed into luxurious accommodations, blending their historical significance with modern amenities. Staying at a masseria offers a glimpse into the region's agrarian past, with opportunities to explore their sprawling grounds and participate in traditional farming activities. Guests can enjoy meals prepared with fresh, local ingredients, often sourced directly from the estate's fields and orchards, creating a true farm-to-table experience.

The architecture of masserie reflects the diverse influences that have shaped Puglia over the centuries. Elements of Byzantine, Norman, and Spanish design can be seen in their construction, illustrating the region's rich tapestry of cultural history. Each masseria has its own unique character, from the elegant courtyards and vaulted ceilings to the rustic stone barns and olive presses. Exploring these historic estates provides a deeper understanding of Puglia's role as a crossroads of civilizations.

Puglia's trulli and masserie are more than just architectural marvels; they are integral to the region's identity and way of life. These structures provide a link to the past, preserving the traditions and craftsmanship that have defined Puglia for generations. They offer a window into the lives of those who have called this land home, from humble farmers to wealthy landowners, each leaving their mark on the landscape.

The preservation and restoration of trulli and masserie are crucial to maintaining Puglia's cultural heritage. Local artisans and craftsmen play a vital role in this process, using traditional techniques and materials to ensure the structures remain true to their origins. This commitment to authenticity is evident in the meticulous care taken to preserve the unique features of each building, from the intricate stonework of the trulli to the imposing facades of the masserie.

For travelers seeking an authentic experience, Puglia's trulli and masserie offer a unique opportunity to connect with the region's history and culture. Whether staying in a beautifully restored trullo or exploring the grounds of a grand masseria, visitors are immersed in the timeless beauty of Puglia's architectural heritage. The stories and traditions of this enchanting region come to life, providing a deeper appreciation for the resilience and creativity of its people.

Puglia's landscape is a canvas painted with the colors of its history, where the whitewashed trulli and stately masserie stand as symbols of a rich and diverse cultural tapestry. The region's architectural wonders invite exploration and discovery, offering a journey through time that captivates the imagination and enriches the soul. As you wander through the Itria Valley and beyond, the allure of Puglia's trulli and masserie beckons, promising an unforgettable experience that lingers long after the journey ends.

5.3. Calabria's Rugged Coastlines

Calabria, the toe of Italy's boot, is a region where dramatic coastlines meet the azure waters of the Mediterranean Sea. This rugged stretch of land, defined by its steep cliffs, hidden coves, and pristine beaches, offers a breathtaking panorama that captivates the senses. The interplay of land and sea creates a landscape of striking beauty, where nature's raw power is on full display, inviting visitors to explore its untamed charm.

The Tyrrhenian coast, with its jagged cliffs and secluded bays, is a testament to Calabria's wild allure. Here, the Costa degli Dei, or "Coast of the Gods," stretches for nearly 55 kilometers, offering some of the most stunning vistas in the region. The town of Tropea, perched high above the sea, is a jewel of this coastline. Known for its picturesque setting and stunning views, Tropea's white sandy beaches and crystal-clear waters are framed by dramatic cliffs that plunge into the sea, creating a natural amphitheater of breathtaking beauty.

Tropea's historic center, with its narrow streets and charming piazzas, invites exploration. The town's cliffside position provides panoramic views of the surrounding coastline, where the interplay of light and shadow on the water creates a mesmerizing spectacle. The Sanctuary of Santa Maria dell'Isola, a medieval church perched on a rocky promontory, is an iconic symbol of Tropea, offering a vantage point that showcases the full splendor of the coast.

Continuing southward, the Capo Vaticano promontory emerges as a striking feature of Calabria's coastline. Renowned for its white granite cliffs and turquoise waters, this area is a haven for snorkelers and divers, with a rich underwater world teeming with marine life. The secluded beaches and hidden coves offer a sense of tranquility and seclusion, where the rhythm of the waves provides a soothing soundtrack to the natural beauty that surrounds you.

The Ionian coast, by contrast, presents a different kind of allure. Here, the coastline stretches in a seemingly endless expanse of sandy beaches and pine forests, where the sea meets the land in a gentle embrace. The ancient town of Gerace, situated on a hill overlooking the coast, provides a window into Calabria's rich history. With its medieval architecture and ancient ruins, Gerace offers a glimpse into a bygone era, where the echoes of past civilizations still resonate.

Further along the Ionian coast lies the town of Scilla, a place steeped in myth and legend. According to ancient tales, Scilla was home to the sea monster Scylla, who terrorized sailors navigating the treacherous waters of the Strait of Messina. Today, Scilla is a charming fishing village, where colorful boats bob in the harbor and the scent of the sea fills the air. The district of Chianalea, known as the "Venice of the South," features narrow alleys and houses that seem to rise from the sea, creating a picturesque setting that captures the imagination.

Calabria's rugged coastlines are also home to a wealth of cultural and natural treasures. The Aspromonte National Park, with its dramatic mountains and diverse ecosystems, offers a stunning backdrop to the coastal landscape. Hiking trails lead through dense forests and open meadows, revealing breathtaking views of the coastline below. The park is a haven for wildlife, with rare species such as the Italian wolf and the Bonelli's eagle finding refuge in its rugged terrain.

The region's culinary traditions are deeply influenced by its coastal setting. Fresh seafood features prominently in Calabrian cuisine, with dishes that showcase the bounty of the Mediterranean. Anchovies, swordfish, and octopus are prepared with simple ingredients, allowing the natural flavors to shine. 'Nduja, a spicy spreadable salami, is a local specialty that adds a fiery kick to many dishes, reflecting the bold and vibrant character of Calabria itself.

Calabria's coastlines are a testament to the region's natural beauty and cultural richness. The interplay of land and sea creates a landscape that is both dramatic and serene, offering a sense of adventure and discovery. Whether exploring the hidden coves of the Tyrrhenian coast or basking in the sun on the sandy beaches of the Ionian shore, visitors are immersed in the timeless beauty of Calabria's rugged coastal landscapes.

The people of Calabria, with their warmth and hospitality, add to the region's allure. Proud of their heritage and deeply connected to the land and sea, the Calabresi welcome visitors with open arms, eager to share the stories and traditions that define their way of life. Whether savoring a homemade meal in a seaside trattoria or engaging in conversation with a local fisherman, the sense of community and connection is palpable, enriching the experience of exploring this remarkable region.

As the sun sets over the horizon, casting a golden glow across the water, the magic of Calabria's coastlines is undeniable. The rugged beauty of the land and the endless expanse of the sea create a sense of wonder and awe, a reminder of nature's enduring power and grace. In Calabria, the coastlines are more than just a backdrop; they are a living, breathing tapestry that invites exploration and reflection, offering a journey into the heart of Italy's untamed beauty.

5.4. Sicily: Ancient Traditions and Modern Flair

Sicily, the largest island in the Mediterranean, stands as a testament to the rich tapestry of cultures that have influenced its history. The island's unique blend of ancient traditions and modern flair creates a vibrant mosaic that captivates all who visit. From the remnants of Greek and Roman civilizations to the bustling markets and contemporary art scenes, Sicily offers a journey through time and a glimpse into the future.

The island's ancient heritage is woven into the very fabric of its landscape. The Valley of the Temples, located near the town of Agrigento, is a breathtaking example of Greek architecture and one of Sicily's most iconic landmarks. These well-preserved Doric temples, set against a backdrop of olive groves and azure skies, transport visitors back to a time when Sicily was a thriving Greek colony. Wandering among the ruins, one can almost hear the echoes of ancient rituals and imagine the grandeur of these sacred spaces.

Beyond the grandeur of Greek temples, Sicily's Roman influence is evident in the intricate mosaics of Villa Romana del Casale. Nestled in the heart of the island, this opulent villa boasts some of the most exquisite Roman mosaics in the world. Each mosaic tells a story, from scenes of mythological gods to depictions of daily life, offering a vivid glimpse into the opulence and sophistication of Roman society. The artistry and craftsmanship on display continue to inspire awe and admiration, bridging the gap between ancient and modern times.

As one delves deeper into Sicily's cultural landscape, the island's diverse traditions come to life. The vibrant streets of Palermo, Sicily's capital, are a sensory feast, where the past and present collide in a whirlwind of colors, sounds, and aromas. The bustling markets, such as Mercato di Ballarò and Mercato di Capo, are alive with the chatter of vendors and the scent of fresh produce, spices, and seafood. Here, the island's culinary heritage unfolds, with influences from Arab, Norman, and Spanish cuisines creating a delectable fusion of flavors.

Sicilian cuisine is a celebration of the island's bountiful land and sea. Dishes such as arancini, caponata, and pasta alla Norma showcase the creativity and resourcefulness of Sicilian cooks, who have mastered the art of transforming simple ingredients into culinary masterpieces. The island's sweets, including cannoli and cassata, are a testament to Sicily's love affair with sugar and citrus, offering a delightful conclusion to any meal.

In the realm of arts and crafts, Sicily continues to honor its traditions while embracing contemporary influences. The town of Caltagirone, known for its vibrant ceramics, is a hub of artistic activity. Here, artisans create intricate pottery and tiles, drawing inspiration from centuries-old techniques and motifs. These colorful creations adorn the island's churches, homes, and public spaces, adding a touch of Sicilian flair to everyday life.

Sicily's modern artistic expression is equally captivating. The island's contemporary art scene is thriving, with galleries and exhibitions showcasing the work of local and international artists. Cities like Palermo and Catania serve as cultural epicenters, where art meets activism, and creativity flourishes amidst the backdrop of historical architecture. Festivals and events, such as the Palermo Pride and Manifesta Biennial, celebrate diversity and innovation, highlighting Sicily's role as a dynamic and evolving cultural crossroads.

As the sun sets over the island, Sicily's nightlife comes alive with a blend of traditional and modern entertainment. From the lively folk music and dance performances in quaint village squares to the vibrant clubs and bars in urban centers, there is something for everyone. The island's festivals, such as the Feast of Santa Rosalia and the Infiorata di Noto, provide a glimpse into the heart of Sicilian community life, where centuries-old customs are celebrated with fervor and joy.

Sicily's natural beauty is as diverse as its cultural heritage. The island's rugged coastline, with its dramatic cliffs and hidden coves, offers a stunning backdrop for exploration and adventure. The majestic Mount Etna, Europe's tallest active volcano, stands as a symbol of the island's fiery spirit, its slopes dotted with vineyards and orchards that benefit from the fertile volcanic soil. Hiking trails and guided tours provide an opportunity to witness the raw power and beauty of this natural wonder.

In contrast, the tranquil landscapes of the Madonie and Nebrodi mountains offer a serene escape, where lush forests and rolling hills invite leisurely walks and picnics. The Aeolian Islands, a volcanic archipelago off the northern coast, beckon with their crystal-clear waters and unique geological formations, providing a paradise for divers and nature enthusiasts.

Sicily's fusion of ancient traditions and modern flair is a reflection of its resilient and adaptive spirit. The island's rich history and cultural diversity have shaped a unique identity, where the past is honored and the future embraced. Whether exploring ancient ruins, savoring culinary delights, or immersing oneself in contemporary art and music, Sicily offers a journey of discovery and connection.

For those seeking to understand the essence of Sicily, the island's people are the true custodians of its heritage. Their warmth, hospitality, and pride in their culture create an inviting atmosphere, where visitors are welcomed as friends and encouraged to share in the island's stories and traditions. Engaging with locals, whether through a spontaneous conversation in a market or a shared meal in a family-run trattoria, provides a deeper insight into the soul of Sicily.

Sicily is a land of contrasts and harmonies, where ancient stones and modern beats coexist in a symphony of life. The island's enduring allure lies in its ability to captivate and inspire, offering a tapestry of experiences that leave an indelible mark on the heart and mind. As the journey through Sicily unfolds, it becomes clear that the island's true magic lies not only in its landscapes and monuments but in the spirit of its people and their unwavering connection to the past and present.

5.5. Sardinia's Interior: A Step Back in Time

Sardinia, an island that rises like a rugged jewel from the Mediterranean, offers an interior landscape that feels like a step back in time. This heartland of the island, away from the sun-kissed beaches and vibrant coastal towns, is a realm where ancient traditions linger and nature reigns supreme. Exploring Sardinia's interior is an invitation to discover its timeless culture, storied past, and unspoiled vistas that stretch as far as the eye can see.

The journey begins with the Nuragic civilization, whose enigmatic stone structures, known as nuraghi, dot the Sardinian landscape. These prehistoric towers, built between 1900 and 730 BCE, are a testament to the ingenuity and resilience of the island's early inhabitants. The Nuraghe Su Nuraxi in Barumini, a UNESCO World Heritage site, stands as a striking example of this ancient architecture. Its massive stone walls and labyrinthine corridors invite exploration, offering a glimpse into the lives and mysteries of a people long gone.

As you venture further into the island's interior, the landscape transforms into a tapestry of rolling hills, dense forests, and dramatic mountain ranges. The Gennargentu National Park, home to Sardinia's highest peaks, presents an untamed wilderness that beckons adventurers and nature lovers alike. Here, hiking trails wind through pristine landscapes, revealing panoramic views of valleys and peaks, where the air is crisp and the silence profound. The park is a sanctuary for wildlife, with golden eagles soaring above and mouflon sheep roaming the rugged terrain.

In the heart of Sardinia, the traditions and customs of the island's people are preserved with a fierce pride. The villages nestled within the mountains are living museums, where the rhythms of rural life continue undisturbed. In places like Orgosolo and Mamoiada, murals adorn the walls, telling stories of struggle, resistance, and community. These vibrant works of art reflect the island's complex history and the indomitable spirit of its people.

Sardinia's interior is also a treasure trove of culinary delights, where age-old recipes are handed down through generations. The island's pastoral heritage is evident in its cuisine, which features robust flavors and simple ingredients. Pecorino sardo, a rich sheep's milk cheese, is a staple of the Sardinian diet, often enjoyed with pane carasau, a thin, crispy bread that has been a symbol of the island's culinary tradition for centuries. The local wines, such as Cannonau and Vermentino, offer a taste of Sardinia's diverse terroir, each sip a reflection of the land's bounty.

The island's festivals provide a window into the vibrant culture of its interior. The Sagra del Redentore, held in Nuoro, is a celebration of religious devotion and communal spirit. Participants, dressed in traditional costumes, gather to honor the statue of Christ the Redeemer, with processions and festivities that bring the community together. The Carnival of Mamoiada, renowned for its haunting Mamuthones and Issohadores masks, is a spectacle of ancient rituals and vibrant pageantry, where the line between past and present blurs in a dance of tradition and mystery.

Sardinia's interior landscape is interwoven with legends and folklore, where the past is always present. The tales of bandits and shepherds, of enchanted forests and mythical creatures, are part of the island's rich oral tradition. These stories, passed down through the generations, offer a glimpse into the soul of Sardinia, where history and myth converge to create a tapestry of intrigue and wonder.

The art of craftsmanship thrives in the island's heartland, where artisans create works that are both beautiful and functional. The weaving of textiles, the crafting of traditional knives, and the production of intricate jewelry are skills honed over centuries. These crafts are not only a means of livelihood but a way of preserving the island's cultural heritage, with each piece embodying the spirit and artistry of Sardinia.

As you explore Sardinia's interior, the hospitality of its people is a constant companion. The Sardinians are known for their warmth and generosity, welcoming visitors with open arms and a genuine curiosity. Sharing a meal with a local family or engaging in conversation over a cup of strong, aromatic coffee provides insight into the island's way of life, where community and connection are cherished above all.

In the quiet of the interior, where time seems to stand still, Sardinia reveals its true essence. The island's rugged beauty and rich history are etched into every stone, every tree, and every face. The land is a living testament to the endurance and adaptability of its people, who have carved out a life in harmony with nature, respecting the legacy of their ancestors while embracing the future.

Sardinia's interior is a journey into the heart of an ancient island, where the past and present coexist in a delicate balance. It is a place of discovery and reflection, where the beauty of the land and the resilience of its people leave an indelible mark on the soul. As the sun sets behind the mountains, casting a golden hue over the landscape, the timeless allure of Sardinia's heartland becomes clear—a reminder of the enduring power of tradition and the beauty of a life lived in harmony with the land.

5.6. The Aeolian Islands: Volcanic Wonders

The Aeolian Islands, a string of volcanic gems scattered across the Tyrrhenian Sea, offer a unique blend of natural beauty and geological intrigue. Named after Aeolus, the Greek god of the winds, these islands have long captivated the imagination of travelers and storytellers alike. Each island possesses its own distinct character, yet together they form a captivating archipelago that is as diverse as it is enchanting.

Stromboli, the most famous of the Aeolian Islands, is known for its active volcano, which has been in almost continuous eruption for over two millennia. The island's dramatic silhouette rises from the sea, a beacon of fiery energy against the sky. Visitors to Stromboli are drawn to its unique volcanic activity, where the "Sciara del Fuoco," a steep slope of black volcanic rock, serves as a natural stage for the frequent explosive eruptions. As night falls, the fiery glow of lava against the dark sky creates a mesmerizing spectacle, an awe-inspiring reminder of the raw power of nature.

The island of Vulcano, named after the Roman god of fire, offers a different volcanic experience. Known for its therapeutic mud baths and fumaroles, Vulcano is a haven for those seeking relaxation and rejuvenation. The island's landscape is characterized by its otherworldly fumaroles, where steam and gases escape from the earth, creating a surreal environment that is both intriguing and soothing. The warm mud baths, rich in minerals, are said to have healing properties, offering a unique way to connect with the island's volcanic essence.

Lipari, the largest of the Aeolian Islands, serves as the archipelago's cultural and economic hub. With its charming streets and vibrant harbor, Lipari is a lively blend of history and modernity. The island's archaeological museum houses a remarkable collection of artifacts that trace the Aeolian Islands' rich history, from prehistoric times to the present day. The ancient acropolis, with its stunning views of the surrounding islands, provides a glimpse into the island's past, where Greek, Roman, and Norman influences have left their mark.

Salina, known for its lush landscapes and verdant vineyards, offers a serene retreat from the bustling activity of its neighboring islands. The island's twin peaks, Monte dei Porri and Monte Fossa delle Felci, dominate the skyline, providing a dramatic backdrop to the fertile valleys below. Salina's fertile soil supports the cultivation of Malvasia grapes, a variety used to produce the island's renowned sweet wine. Tasting this wine is a journey into the island's terroir, where the unique volcanic soil imparts a distinct flavor to the grapes.

Panarea, the smallest and most exclusive of the Aeolian Islands, is a playground for the rich and famous. Despite its small size, Panarea boasts a vibrant social scene, with chic boutiques, upscale restaurants, and a lively nightlife. The island's pristine beaches and azure waters provide a stunning setting for relaxation and luxury, where the pace of life slows down and the beauty of the surroundings takes center stage. For those seeking a touch of glamour amidst natural beauty, Panarea offers a perfect escape.

Filicudi and Alicudi, the westernmost islands of the archipelago, offer a glimpse into a simpler, more traditional way of life. These islands, with their rugged landscapes and charming villages, are a haven for nature lovers and adventurers. Hiking trails wind through the islands' untamed terrain, revealing breathtaking views of the sea and sky. The sense of isolation and tranquility is palpable, providing a stark contrast to the bustling activity of the more populated islands. For those seeking solitude and connection with nature, Filicudi and Alicudi offer an unspoiled paradise.

The Aeolian Islands' volcanic origins have shaped not only their landscapes but also their culture and traditions. The islanders have long lived in harmony with the volcanic forces that define their home, adapting their way of life to the rhythms of nature. The islands' cuisine reflects this connection, with dishes that celebrate the bounty of the sea and the richness of the soil. Fresh seafood, capers, and locally grown produce feature prominently in Aeolian dishes, offering a taste of the islands' vibrant flavors.

Exploring the Aeolian Islands is a journey through a world where time seems to stand still, and the wonders of nature are ever-present. The islands' volcanic landscapes, with their dramatic cliffs, black sand beaches, and steaming fumaroles, create a sense of awe and wonder. Whether hiking up Stromboli's fiery slopes, soaking in Vulcano's soothing mud baths, or savoring a glass of Malvasia wine, visitors are immersed in the islands' unique blend of natural beauty and cultural richness.

The Aeolian Islands' allure lies in their ability to captivate and inspire, offering a tapestry of experiences that leave a lasting impression. Each island, with its own distinct character and charm, invites exploration and discovery, providing a window into the timeless beauty of this volcanic archipelago. As the sun sets over the Tyrrhenian Sea, casting a golden glow across the water, the magic of the Aeolian Islands becomes clear—a reminder of the enduring power of nature and the beauty of life in harmony with the earth.

6. PRACTICAL TIPS FOR AUTHENTIC ITALIAN EXPERIENCES

6.1. Connecting with Locals

Meeting and connecting with locals is one of the most rewarding aspects of traveling. It allows you to delve deeper into the culture, understand the nuances of everyday life, and gain insights that go beyond the typical tourist experience. In many ways, locals are the true ambassadors of their homeland, offering authentic perspectives and stories that enrich your journey. Building these connections requires openness, curiosity, and respect for the customs and traditions of the place you are visiting.

One of the most effective ways to connect with locals is through language. Even a few basic phrases in the local tongue can open doors and hearts. Greetings, expressions of gratitude, and simple questions in the native language demonstrate a genuine interest in the culture and a willingness to step outside your comfort zone. Language barriers can be daunting, but they also present opportunities for creativity and humor, often leading to memorable interactions. A smile, a gesture, or a shared laugh can transcend words, forging connections that resonate on a human level.

Participating in local events and festivals is another excellent way to engage with residents. These gatherings, whether religious, cultural, or seasonal, provide a window into the community's values and traditions. Joining in the festivities allows you to experience the vibrancy and spirit of the local culture firsthand. Whether it's dancing in a village square, savoring traditional dishes at a food festival, or witnessing a time-honored ritual, these moments create shared experiences that foster a sense of belonging and camaraderie.

Staying in locally-owned accommodations, such as guesthouses, homestays, or small boutique hotels, can also facilitate meaningful interactions. These settings often encourage a more personal connection with hosts, who are usually eager to share their knowledge and insights about the area. Your hosts can offer recommendations for off-the-beaten-path attractions, introduce you to local customs, and provide a glimpse into daily life. The warmth and hospitality extended by these hosts often leave a lasting impression, creating bonds that extend beyond your stay.

Engaging with the local culinary scene is yet another avenue for building connections. Food is a universal language that brings people together, and sharing a meal with locals can be a powerful way to learn about their culture. Visiting markets, dining at family-run eateries, or attending cooking classes allows you to interact with residents and learn about the ingredients and techniques that define the local cuisine. These experiences offer a taste of authenticity, where stories of family recipes and culinary traditions add depth to the flavors on your plate.

Volunteering or participating in community projects provides a unique opportunity to contribute to the places you visit while connecting with locals on a deeper level. Whether it's helping with conservation efforts, teaching languages, or supporting local artisans, these activities foster a sense of purpose and connection. Volunteering allows you to engage with residents in meaningful ways, offering a chance to learn from one another and build bridges across cultural divides.

Approaching interactions with locals requires sensitivity and respect. It's important to be mindful of cultural norms and etiquette, as well as to approach conversations with genuine curiosity and an open mind. Listening is as crucial as speaking, as it demonstrates respect and a willingness to learn from those you meet. Asking thoughtful questions and showing an interest in local life can lead to enriching dialogues and shared insights.

While technology can facilitate connections, it's essential to strike a balance between online and offline interactions. Social media platforms and travel forums can be useful tools for connecting with locals before and during your trip, offering opportunities to learn about the culture and seek recommendations. However, it's important to prioritize face-to-face interactions, as these moments often lead to the most authentic and memorable experiences.

The benefits of connecting with locals extend beyond the immediate travel experience. These interactions can lead to lasting friendships, offering a network of connections that span the globe. They provide a deeper understanding of the world and its diverse cultures, fostering empathy and appreciation for the shared human experience. As you return home, the stories and memories of your encounters with locals become cherished souvenirs, enriching your life long after the journey has ended.

For those seeking to make the most of their travels, connecting with locals is an invaluable element of the experience. It transforms a trip from a series of sights and activities into a journey of discovery and connection. By embracing the opportunity to engage with the people who call your destination home, you gain a richer, more nuanced understanding of the world and your place within it. Through these connections, the world becomes a smaller, more interconnected place, where the bonds of friendship and shared humanity transcend borders and cultures.

6.2. Using Technology to Discover Hidden Gems

In an era where technology permeates every facet of our lives, its influence on travel has been nothing short of transformative. The once-daunting task of uncovering hidden gems in unfamiliar destinations is now made easier with the help of digital tools. From apps that map out obscure attractions to platforms that connect you with local insights, technology has opened a world of possibilities for those seeking unique experiences.

Smartphone applications are at the forefront of this revolution, offering a plethora of options to explore off-the-beaten-path locales. Apps like Google Maps have evolved to do more than just provide directions; they offer user-generated content, highlighting lesser-known spots that might otherwise be overlooked. By reading reviews and examining photos shared by fellow travelers, you can discover that tucked-away café or secluded beach that isn't featured in mainstream travel guides.

Social media platforms, particularly Instagram and Pinterest, serve as visual diaries, capturing the beauty of hidden gems through the eyes of those who have stumbled upon them. Searching for hashtags related to your destination can lead you to stunning visuals and recommendations for places you might not have considered. The real-time nature of these platforms ensures that the information is current, allowing you to adjust your itinerary based on recent discoveries.

Travel blogs and forums provide another treasure trove of information, often penned by passionate explorers who relish in revealing their best finds. Websites such as TripAdvisor and Lonely Planet host forums where travelers exchange tips and stories. These narratives often include personal recommendations for unique experiences, from quaint villages to local festivals, that might not be well-documented elsewhere. Engaging with these communities can provide a wealth of knowledge and inspire you to venture beyond the usual tourist track.

Augmented reality (AR) applications are also making waves, offering interactive experiences that bring history and culture to life. By overlaying digital information onto the physical world, AR apps can provide insights into the hidden stories behind a seemingly ordinary street or building. This technology enhances your understanding of a place, revealing layers of history and significance that deepen your appreciation.

When seeking hidden gems, technology-driven experiences can be further enriched by connecting with locals through various platforms. Websites like Couchsurfing and Meetup offer opportunities to engage with residents who are eager to share their favorite spots. These interactions provide a more authentic experience, as locals often have insider knowledge of the best-kept secrets in their area. Whether it's a family-run restaurant with homemade specialties or a hidden hiking trail with breathtaking views, locals can guide you to places that resonate with the heart and soul of their community.

Incorporating technology into your travel plans also allows for greater flexibility and spontaneity. With mobile apps and online resources at your fingertips, you can adapt to changing circumstances and seize opportunities as they arise. Whether it's an unexpected recommendation from a fellow traveler or a sudden change in weather, technology provides the tools to pivot and make the most of your journey.

However, it's important to strike a balance between digital exploration and real-world experiences. While technology can guide you to hidden gems, the most memorable discoveries often happen when you allow yourself to wander and explore without a set agenda. Embrace serendipity by taking a detour down a side street or striking up a conversation with a local. These moments of unplanned exploration can lead to the most rewarding experiences, where the true essence of a place is revealed.

In the quest to uncover hidden gems, technology serves as a powerful ally, opening doors to experiences that might otherwise remain out of reach. Yet, it is the combination of digital tools and human curiosity that truly enriches the journey. By leveraging technology alongside a spirit of adventure, you can uncover the hidden wonders that make each destination uniquely captivating. Through this harmonious blend, travel becomes not just a series of sights, but a tapestry of discoveries that linger long after the journey ends.

6.3. Seasonal Events and Festivals

Italy is a country where the rhythm of life is punctuated by a rich tapestry of seasonal events and festivals. Each region showcases its unique traditions, drawing visitors into a world of vibrant colors, lively music, and tantalizing flavors. These festivals provide a window into the heart of Italian culture, offering experiences that go beyond the typical tourist trails. Attending these events is more than just participating in a celebration; it's about immersing oneself in the local way of life, understanding the deep-seated customs, and forming genuine connections with the people.

One of the most famous events that heralds the arrival of spring is the Carnevale di Venezia. This iconic festival, with its origins in the 12th century, is renowned for its elaborate masks and opulent costumes. As you wander through the labyrinthine streets of Venice, you'll encounter street performers, musicians, and theatrical events that transform the city into a grand stage. The energy is palpable, and the sense of history is ever-present as you partake in the masquerade balls and witness the grand parades that float along the canals.

Traveling south to Florence, the Scoppio del Carro marks Easter with a bang— literally. This centuries-old tradition involves a grand procession leading to a spectacular display of fireworks, ignited from a cart pulled by white oxen. The event symbolizes peace and prosperity, and the vibrant explosion of colors against the backdrop of Florence's historic architecture is a sight to behold. For those seeking a more intimate experience, consider attending the smaller, lesser-known Easter processions in the hilltop towns of Tuscany, where the community gathers in a display of solemnity and faith.

As the summer heat envelops the country, the Palio di Siena takes center stage. This medieval horse race, held in the Piazza del Campo, is a fierce competition between Siena's districts, or contrade. The passionate rivalry is evident in the elaborate pageantry and fervent cheers of the crowd. Witnessing the race is a thrilling experience, but the true essence of the event is felt in the days leading up to it, as each contrada hosts feasts and celebrations, inviting outsiders to partake in their traditions.

In the coastal town of Amalfi, the Regata delle Antiche Repubbliche Marinare is a historical reenactment that celebrates Italy's maritime prowess. This rowing race, held every four years, sees crews from Amalfi, Pisa, Genoa, and Venice compete in traditional galleons. The event is steeped in history, with participants donning period costumes and parading through the town, offering a glimpse into the maritime heritage that shaped these cities.

Autumn brings with it the grape harvest, or vendemmia, a time of celebration in wine-producing regions such as Tuscany, Piedmont, and Veneto. Many vineyards open their doors to visitors, offering the opportunity to participate in the grape picking and stomping, a tradition that has been handed down through generations. The harvest culminates in lively festivals, where locals and visitors alike can enjoy the fruits of their labor with wine tastings, music, and feasting.

For those with a sweet tooth, the Eurochocolate festival in Perugia is a must-visit. Held in October, this event transforms the city into a chocolate lover's paradise, with artisans from around the world showcasing their creations. From chocolate sculptures to tastings and workshops, it's a sensory delight that draws chocolate enthusiasts from all corners of the globe.

Winter in Italy is marked by the warmth of Christmas markets and the anticipation of the New Year. The Mercatini di Natale, or Christmas markets, are held in towns and cities across the country, offering handcrafted gifts, local delicacies, and festive cheer. Bolzano, in the heart of the South Tyrol, is home to one of the most enchanting markets, where the alpine atmosphere adds a magical touch to the holiday season.

In the historic city of Naples, the living nativity scenes, or presepi viventi, are a cherished tradition. Families and communities come together to recreate the nativity scene with intricate detail, often incorporating elements of Neapolitan culture and daily life. This unique blend of religious devotion and artistic expression is a testament to the creativity and spirit of the people.

The arrival of the new year is celebrated with the Festa di San Silvestro, where Italians gather for a grand feast, culminating in a midnight toast with prosecco. In Rome, the festivities spill onto the streets, with fireworks illuminating the sky over the Colosseum and music filling the air. It's a time of joy and optimism, as families and friends come together to welcome the year ahead.

To truly embrace these seasonal events and festivals, it's important to approach them with an open heart and a willingness to engage with the locals. Strike up conversations, ask questions, and be receptive to the stories and customs that are shared. By doing so, you'll discover the warmth and hospitality that define the Italian spirit, and you'll leave with memories that resonate long after the celebration has ended.

6.4. Nightlife Beyond the Tourist Areas

Venturing into the heart of Italy's nightlife offers an authentic glimpse into a world that tourists rarely experience. Beyond the well-trodden paths of bustling city centers, a vibrant tapestry of local haunts, intimate music venues, and cozy enotecas awaits. These are the places where the soul of Italy truly thrives after the sun has set, offering an unfiltered taste of the culture and camaraderie that defines Italian social life.

In Rome, stepping away from the crowds of Via del Corso and Piazza di Spagna reveals the district of Pigneto. Once a working-class neighborhood, Pigneto has transformed into a hub of creativity and bohemian spirit. The streets here are lined with quirky bars, each with its distinct character. At night, the area comes alive with the chatter of locals filling the air as they gather for aperitivo. It's in these small, dimly lit bars where you'll find jazz performances and indie bands playing to intimate crowds, creating an atmosphere that's both electric and welcoming.

Florence's nightlife offers a different kind of allure. While the city is known for its renaissance art and architecture, its Oltrarno district is where you'll discover the artisans of today. As day turns to night, the workshops close, and the streets come alive with the hum of conversations spilling out from the small wine bars and trattorias. Here, you can enjoy a glass of Chianti while listening to live performances of traditional Tuscan folk music, often accompanied by spontaneous dancing. The sense of community is palpable, and visitors are often welcomed as friends rather than tourists.

For those seeking a coastal vibe, the city of Genoa offers a blend of maritime history and vibrant nightlife. The narrow alleyways of the historic center, known as caruggi, house hidden gems—speakeasies that whisper stories of the past and bars that serve up unique cocktails inspired by the sea. The locals here are passionate about their city, and striking up a conversation can lead to fascinating insights into Genoa's rich history and culture. As the evening progresses, head to the waterfront where the sound of waves accompanies live music under the stars.

Naples, a city renowned for its chaotic energy and culinary delights, offers a nightlife experience that is as spirited as its people. Venturing into the Spanish Quarters reveals a labyrinth of streets where locals gather in small, unassuming bars. These are places where you can enjoy a Neapolitan craft beer or a simple yet perfect glass of limoncello. The music ranges from traditional tarantella to modern Neapolitan pop, and the mood is always lively. Embracing the spontaneity of Naples means you might find yourself joining the locals in a late-night promenade along the Lungomare, with the imposing silhouette of Mount Vesuvius as your backdrop.

In the heart of Sicily, Palermo's nightlife is a reflection of its diverse cultural influences. The Vucciria market, during the day a bustling hub of food vendors, transforms at night into a lively scene of street performances and open-air bars. Here, you can savor the flavors of Sicily with a plate of arancini in one hand and a glass of local wine in the other. The music is as varied as the island's history, with Arabic, Norman, and Spanish influences creating a unique soundscape. Engaging with the locals often leads to impromptu lessons in Sicilian dialect, adding a layer of authenticity to the experience.

In the smaller towns and villages of Italy, nightlife often centers around the piazza, the beating heart of community life. These are places where time seems to slow down, and the simple pleasure of enjoying gelato while sitting on a stone bench is cherished. The conversations are often punctuated by laughter, and the sense of belonging is strong. These gatherings are not about the spectacle; they are about connection and the shared experience of being part of a community.

To truly embrace Italy's nightlife beyond the tourist areas, it's important to adopt the local rhythm. Start your evening with an aperitivo, a pre-dinner drink that serves as both a social ritual and a way to unwind. When dining, seek out trattorias and osterias frequented by locals, where the menu is often dictated by what's fresh and in season. After dinner, take your time to explore the area, allowing yourself to be guided by the sounds of music and laughter.

Engaging with locals is key to discovering hidden nightlife gems. Don't hesitate to ask for recommendations; Italians take pride in their local haunts and are often eager to share their favorite spots. Whether it's a secluded bar tucked away in a side street or a basement club hosting an underground dance party, locals can provide insights that guidebooks simply cannot.

Ultimately, the essence of Italy's nightlife is found in its authenticity. It's about connecting with the people, savoring the moment, and embracing the unexpected. By stepping away from the tourist areas and into the local scene, you'll uncover a side of Italy that's rich with stories, flavors, and unforgettable experiences.

6.5. Shopping Like a Local

Shopping like a local offers a unique opportunity to immerse yourself in the culture of a destination, providing insights into the everyday lives of its residents. Unlike the predictable experience of global chain stores and tourist-focused markets, local shopping experiences are filled with character, tradition, and the charm of discovering something truly special. By stepping away from the familiar and exploring the local retail scene, you gain access to authentic products, traditional craftsmanship, and a deeper understanding of the community's way of life.

One of the most rewarding ways to shop like a local is by visiting markets that cater primarily to residents. These markets, bustling with activity and vibrant with color, often form the heart of a community. Here, vendors sell fresh produce, handmade goods, and artisanal products that reflect the region's unique culture and traditions. Engaging with market vendors provides a chance to learn about local ingredients, cooking techniques, and the stories behind the products they sell. As you sample regional delicacies or admire the craftsmanship of handmade items, you gain a connection to the people and the land.

Specialty shops and boutiques also offer a window into the local culture. These establishments, often family-owned, provide a carefully curated selection of products that highlight the region's artistry and heritage. Whether it's a boutique featuring contemporary local fashion, a shop specializing in traditional crafts, or a store offering locally produced gourmet foods, these places provide an intimate shopping experience. The owners and staff are often passionate about their offerings, eager to share the history and significance of each item with curious customers.

Exploring second-hand and vintage stores is another way to shop like a local. These stores, filled with treasures from the past, offer a glimpse into the history and tastes of the community. Whether you're searching for a unique piece of clothing, a rare vinyl record, or an antique piece of furniture, these shops provide an eclectic mix of items that tell stories of bygone eras. The thrill of the hunt and the joy of discovering something unexpected make these shopping excursions memorable and rewarding.

Local shopping experiences are not just about the goods you purchase; they're about the connections you make along the way. Striking up conversations with shopkeepers, artisans, and fellow shoppers can lead to enriching exchanges and valuable insights. Asking for recommendations, whether for other shops, local eateries, or hidden attractions, often uncovers gems that aren't listed in guidebooks. These interactions add depth to your understanding of the community and create memorable moments that stay with you long after your trip.

To truly shop like a local, it's important to be mindful of the cultural norms and practices in the area. Observing how locals interact in these settings can provide clues about etiquette, bargaining practices, and payment methods. In some cultures, bargaining is expected and can be a friendly and engaging part of the shopping experience. In others, prices are fixed, and haggling may be seen as disrespectful. Being aware of these nuances ensures a respectful and enjoyable shopping experience for everyone involved.

Supporting local businesses and artisans by purchasing their goods contributes to the economic sustainability of the community. By choosing to buy local, you help preserve traditional crafts and support the livelihoods of those who dedicate their lives to their craft. This commitment to sustainable shopping reflects a deeper respect for the culture you are experiencing and fosters a sense of connection to the people and the place.

While shopping, consider seeking out unique, locally-made souvenirs that capture the essence of the destination. These items, whether they are handcrafted jewelry, local textiles, or specialty foods, serve as tangible reminders of your journey. They carry with them the stories of the artisans who created them and the cultural heritage they represent. As you bring these treasures home, they become part of your own story, evoking memories of the experiences and connections made along the way.

Shopping like a local encourages a slower, more thoughtful approach to travel. It invites you to wander through neighborhoods, explore side streets, and take the time to appreciate the details that define a community. This method of exploration often leads to unexpected discoveries, where the joy lies not just in the destination, but in the journey itself.

Ultimately, shopping like a local is about embracing the authenticity of a place and engaging with it on a personal level. It transforms a simple transaction into a meaningful exchange, where the value lies not just in the item purchased, but in the experience and connections formed. As you explore the local shopping scene, you gain a deeper appreciation for the craftsmanship, creativity, and cultural richness that define the community, creating lasting memories and a sense of belonging that extends beyond your travels.

6.6. Dealing with Unexpected Situations

Traveling is an adventure that promises new experiences, but it can also bring its share of surprises and unexpected situations. Handling these moments with grace and adaptability is key to a rewarding journey. While meticulous planning can reduce the likelihood of unforeseen events, it is impossible to control every aspect of a trip. Therefore, being prepared to handle surprises is crucial for a smooth and enjoyable experience.

One of the most common unexpected situations travelers face is flight delays or cancellations. These disruptions can throw a wrench in your plans, but maintaining composure is essential. The first step is to stay informed by checking flight statuses regularly through airline apps or notifications. In the case of a delay or cancellation, promptly contacting the airline's customer service can help secure alternative arrangements. Maintaining flexibility in your itinerary allows you to adjust plans without significant disappointment. Consider having a few backup activities in mind, or use this time to explore the airport's amenities or nearby attractions.

Lost luggage is another frequent hiccup that can occur during travel. To mitigate its impact, pack essential items in your carry-on, such as a change of clothes, toiletries, and any necessary medications. In the event your luggage goes missing, report it to the airline immediately and provide them with your contact information and a detailed description of the bags. Many airlines offer compensation for essentials until your luggage is returned. Using a tracking device in your luggage can also offer peace of mind, allowing you to monitor its location through your smartphone.

Navigating language barriers can present challenges, especially when visiting countries where you are unfamiliar with the local language. Learning a few key phrases before your trip can facilitate communication and demonstrate respect for the local culture. Carrying a translation app or a pocket phrasebook can also prove invaluable. In situations where language is a barrier, non-verbal communication, such as gestures or visuals, can help bridge the gap and convey your message effectively.

Health-related issues can arise unexpectedly during travel, ranging from minor ailments to more serious conditions. Ensuring you have comprehensive travel insurance before embarking on your journey provides a safety net in case of medical emergencies. It is also wise to carry a basic first-aid kit with essentials like band-aids, antiseptic wipes, and any personal medications. Familiarizing yourself with local healthcare facilities and understanding how to access them in an emergency can alleviate stress and ensure timely medical attention if needed.

Weather conditions can be unpredictable and may impact your plans. Preparing for a range of weather scenarios by packing versatile clothing and gear can help you adapt to changing conditions. If outdoor activities are affected by weather, have a list of indoor alternatives, such as museums or cultural centers, to ensure your day remains fulfilling. Embracing the unexpected and finding joy in alternative experiences can turn what seems like an obstacle into a memorable adventure.

While theft or loss of personal belongings is a distressing possibility, taking precautions can minimize risk. Using a money belt or secure pouch to store important documents, credit cards, and cash can deter pickpockets. Keep photocopies or digital backups of your passport, identification, and travel documents in a secure location. In the unfortunate event of theft, reporting the incident to local authorities and your consulate can expedite the recovery process or replacement of stolen items.

Cultural misunderstandings are another potential source of unexpected situations. Researching cultural norms and etiquette before your trip can prevent inadvertent offenses. Observing and mimicking local behavior in social settings can also guide your interactions. If a misunderstanding does occur, a sincere apology and willingness to learn can go a long way in resolving the issue and fostering goodwill.

Transportation strikes or public transit disruptions may alter your travel plans. Staying informed about local news and transit updates is essential for navigating these situations. Exploring alternative modes of transportation, such as rideshares, bikes, or walking, can offer new perspectives on a destination. Engaging with locals for advice on the best ways to get around can also lead to valuable insights and alternative routes.

Financial mishaps, such as lost or blocked credit cards, can create stress during travel. Carrying multiple forms of payment, such as a backup credit card or sufficient cash, provides a safety net. Informing your bank of your travel plans before departing can prevent unexpected card blocks. In the event of a lost card, most banks offer emergency services to access funds or provide a replacement quickly.

Ultimately, dealing with unexpected situations requires a mindset of adaptability and problem-solving. Viewing challenges as opportunities for growth and discovery can transform your travel experience. Every journey holds the potential for surprises, and how you respond defines the narrative of your adventure. By embracing the unexpected and maintaining a positive outlook, you create space for serendipitous moments that enrich your travels and broaden your perspective. Each challenge overcome becomes a story to share, a testament to your resilience, and a reminder of the dynamic and ever-changing tapestry of the world.

6.7. Resources for Further Exploration

Embarking on an Italian adventure is like opening a doorway to limitless discovery. To truly delve into the heart of this enchanting country, having the right resources at your fingertips is invaluable. These tools not only enhance the experience but also guide you into less-traveled territories, offering a more profound understanding of Italy's many facets. Whether you're a first-time visitor or a seasoned traveler, knowing where to look and whom to follow can transform your journey into an authentic exploration.

One of the essential resources for travelers looking to experience Italy authentically is the wealth of local blogs and online forums. These platforms are often curated by passionate residents who share insider tips, hidden gems, and personal stories. Websites like "Italy Chronicles" provide articles on everything from regional cuisine to cultural nuances, written by those who have lived and breathed Italian life. Engaging with online forums, such as the Italy section on TripAdvisor or Lonely Planet's Thorn Tree, can connect you with fellow travelers and locals eager to share firsthand experiences and advice.

For those who prefer a more tactile approach, guidebooks remain a trusted companion. While mainstream options like Rick Steves' Italy or Lonely Planet cover the essentials, seeking out niche publications can reveal lesser-known treasures. Books dedicated to specific regions or interests, such as "The Food Lover's Guide to Florence" or "Hidden Tuscany," offer deeper insights into local culture and attractions beyond the usual tourist spots. These guides often include itineraries that lead you to quaint villages, artisanal markets, and family-run establishments, ensuring a more personalized encounter with Italy.

Language resources are invaluable for anyone wishing to engage more deeply with the culture. While English is widely spoken in tourist areas, venturing into more rural or traditional locales often requires a basic understanding of Italian.

Language apps such as Duolingo or Babbel offer convenient ways to learn on the go, while phrasebooks can provide quick assistance. Making an effort to speak the local language, even if it's just a few words, is often met with appreciation and can open doors to more genuine interactions.

To uncover Italy's vibrant arts and cultural scene, staying informed about local events is paramount. Websites like "Eventbrite" or "What's On In Italy" list upcoming festivals, exhibitions, and performances across the country. For more local-specific insights, city tourism websites or regional cultural associations often publish monthly calendars highlighting unique activities and seasonal celebrations. Attending these events can provide an immersive experience, allowing you to witness local traditions and artistry firsthand.

Social media platforms, particularly Instagram and Pinterest, are treasure troves of inspiration and information. Following travel influencers and photographers who specialize in Italian content can introduce you to stunning landscapes, architectural marvels, and culinary delights. These visual tools not only inspire but also offer practical advice on locations worth visiting and the best times to do so. Hashtags such as #ItalyHiddenGems or #AuthenticItaly can lead you to posts that showcase off-the-beaten-path experiences shared by travelers who have ventured beyond the usual routes.

For those interested in Italy's culinary riches, connecting with local food tours or cooking classes is a must. Organizations like "Eating Italy" or "Walks of Italy" offer guided experiences that take you into the heart of Italy's culinary traditions. These tours often include visits to local markets, tastings at family-run trattorias, and hands-on cooking sessions where you can learn to make regional specialties. Such activities not only satisfy the palate but also provide a deeper understanding of the cultural significance behind Italy's diverse cuisine.

Engaging with local communities through volunteer opportunities is another way to enrich your Italian experience. Programs like WWOOF Italy (World Wide Opportunities on Organic Farms) allow travelers to work on organic farms in exchange for room and board, offering a unique chance to live and work alongside Italians in rural settings. This immersive experience provides insight into traditional agricultural practices and a chance to contribute positively to the communities you visit.

Transportation resources can also enhance your journey, especially when exploring rural areas or small towns. Websites like Trainline or Trenitalia offer information on train schedules and routes, making it easy to plan travel between cities. For more remote destinations, car rental services such as Europcar or Hertz provide the flexibility to explore at your own pace, allowing you to reach places that are often overlooked by public transport.

Lastly, connecting with local tour guides can personalize your experience. Certified guides bring history and culture to life with their knowledge and storytelling. They can tailor tours to your interests, whether it's exploring ancient ruins, wandering through vineyards, or delving into the art world. Platforms like "Tours By Locals" or "Viator" connect travelers with local experts who can offer personalized, in-depth tours that highlight the unique aspects of each region.

By utilizing these resources, your Italian journey becomes more than just a visit—it transforms into an exploration filled with authenticity and depth. Opening yourself to these tools and connections expands your understanding and appreciation of this remarkable country, creating memories that linger long after the journey has ended.

BONUS 1: 10 TRAVEL TIPS "THAT CAN SAVE THE DAY" DURING AN ITALIAN ADVENTURE

BONUS 2: 50 ESSENTIAL ITALIAN PHRASES FOR YOUR DAILY TRAVEL NEEDS

BONUS 3: PRINTABLE TRAVEL JOURNAL